E-Innovation

Bob Cotton

T0341415

■ Fast track route to successful innovation in a digital world

■ Covers the key areas of e-innovation, from planning for continuous change and trend forecasting to e-innovation processes and distributed innovation

■ Examples and lessons from some of the world's most innovative businesses, including Napster, Cybiko, RedHat, Handspring and Sony, and ideas from the smartest thinkers, including
Eric S. Raymond, James F. Moore, Leonard Fuld, Robert G. Cooper, Peter Small, Bruce Kogut and Anca Meitu

■ Includes a glossary of key concepts and a comprehensive resources guide

≫EXPRESS EXEC.COM≪
essential management thinking at your fingertips

Copyright © Capstone Publishing 2002

The right of Bob Cotton to be identified as the author of this work has been asserted in accordance with the Copyright, Designs and Patents Act 1988

First published 2002 by
Capstone Publishing (A Wiley Company)
8 Newtec Place
Magdalen Road
Oxford OX4 1RE
United Kingdom
http://www.capstoneideas.com

CIP catalogue records for this book are available from the British Library and the US Library of Congress

ISBN 1-84112-240-8

Substantial discounts on bulk quantities of Capstone books are available to corporations, professional associations and other organizations. Please contact Capstone for more details on +44 (0)1865 798 623 or (fax) +44 (0)1865 240 941 or (e-mail) info@wiley-capstone.co.uk

Contents

Introduction to ExpressExec

ExpressExec is 3 million words of the latest management thinking compiled into 10 modules. Each module contains 10 individual titles forming a comprehensive resource of current business practice written by leading practitioners in their field. From brand management to balanced scorecard, ExpressExec enables you to grasp the key concepts behind each subject and implement the theory immediately. Each of the 100 titles is available in print and electronic formats.

Through the ExpressExec.com Website you will discover that you can access the complete resource in a number of ways:

» printed books or e-books;
» e-content – PDF or XML (for licensed syndication) adding value to an intranet or Internet site;
» a corporate e-learning/knowledge management solution providing a cost-effective platform for developing skills and sharing knowledge within an organization;
» bespoke delivery – tailored solutions to solve your need.

Why not visit www.expressexec.com and register for free key management briefings, a monthly newsletter and interactive skills checklists. Share your ideas about ExpressExec and your thoughts about business today.

Please contact elound@wiley-capstone.co.uk for more information.

Introduction to E-Innovation

» Innovation in a rapidly evolving marketplace
» The emergence of e-innovation as a strategy for continuous innovation.

Now that "The Future" is being rolled out in real time, and we barely have time to catch breath before another round of breakthrough technologies emerge, it has become really obvious that we live in a era of continuous innovation. There is an unparalleled range of computing, information-processing, consumer electronics, and media and telecommunication technologies in continuous, across-the-board development, with each new gizmo striving to grow and prosper in the increasingly complex, rapidly changing "ecosystem" of the new networked marketplace.

But marketplaces have always been the product of networks – invisible networks of exchange and commerce: networks of buyers, sellers, manufacturers, collectors, distributors, importers, exporters, money-lenders, law-enforcers, and people just hanging around talking to each other. All these forces have always interacted in the marketplace. And the new networked marketplace is no different from all marketplaces that have ever existed. All markets are always in a state of continuous flux.

So what's so "new" about *Now*? What's so new is the *speed of light*. The invisible communications networks that center on each one of us and that coalesce in marketplaces have now been embodied in telecommunications networks, specifically in electromagnetic pulses, carried by wires, fibers, cables and by space itself all around the world.

And these light-speed networks now carry our conversations and transactions as digital data – the binary 0s and 1s expressed as patterns of pulses, read and interpreted into speech, pictures, and sounds by computers. What's new is that these networks bind us all into real-time simultaneity and what Frances Cairncross calls "the Death of Distance". The sense, and the actuality, of the electronic proximity created by global interpersonal communications have created the new, globally networked marketplace. It's a marketplace where its easier to buy a book from a warehouse in Seattle, or wherever, than it is to pop down to the local bookstore.

As Herbert Marshall McLuhan observed back in the 1960s, we have extruded our central nervous system out into the world, and we now see, hear, and speak intimately with friends, colleagues, and customers all around our global village.

With millions of people, and millions of machines, and hundreds of thousands of businesses interconnected in this vast, light-speed, pulsing network, it's not surprising that change is continuous, or that change is accelerating too. Not only are we constantly inventing the means to send more information through the existing telecommunications networks, we are creating new high-bandwidth networks. New LEO (low-earth orbit) satellite constellations, new 3G cellular networks, new fiber-coax networks, new DSL (digital subscriber loop) telephone networks – all these expand communications from voice through text and graphics to television-quality video, and promise the imminent arrival of 3D virtual realities and other virtual meeting places.

But it's not just the quality, it's the width too – more and more people join this electronic digital network every day. And as Internet pioneer Bob Metcalfe pointed out a few years ago, a network's value increases by the square of the number of people in it. Each new individual – each new "node" amplifies the network's value to everyone else. The more people there are on the Net, the more shops and the more businesses emerge to service them, and the networked digital marketplace becomes a complex engine of accelerating change.

In this climate of continuous radical change, the process of design, strategic planning, and new product development has necessarily had to change and adapt, and the resulting convergence of design, planning, scenario building, technology forecasting, market intelligence, new product development and creative business development is converging into a new, proactive response to change that we can call "e-innovation".

Definition of Terms:
What is E-Innovation?

Change in the electronic marketplace is driven by software. There are acute shortages of software engineers. As a result, new processes of software development are emerging.

» These include outsourcing and open sourcing
» Similar processes are being developed for distributed innovation
» E-innovation is an emerging discipline for proactively responding to change
» It combines strategic planning, design and new product development.

That the growth of personal computing, the Web/Net, cellular and satellite telecommunications networks, and consumer-friendly data-access devices have together created a radically new environment for us all is now all too obvious. The importance of this proliferation of processing power and networks has been likened to the impact of the moveable typeface in the fifteenth century, or to the impact of the industrial revolution in the eighteenth and nineteenth centuries. But the impact of these new technologies promises to be much greater than either of these two world-changing developments. What we are inventing and producing now are technologies that promise new forms of collaborative thinking, and new ways of personally and corporately processing and managing information – as well as an astonishing global electronic marketplace. The intellectual augmentations offered by these new tools of the computer and the Web/Net are transforming our world. These are the tools that underpin virtually all creative developments all over the world – in the biological sciences, in physics, in industry, in medicine, in agriculture, and in governance. It's already obvious that the computer and the Web/Net are determining the future of money, education, business, media distribution, telecommunications, and entertainment. The impact of the developing ICT (information and communication) technologies, as they ramify through every aspect of our lives, is affecting everything.

It will obviously take a considerable time for the implications of massively networked media, abundant personal information processing power, and intimate global personal communications to become clear, and in the meantime we have to develop the best tools that we can to evolve heuristics, tactics and strategies with which to plan our personal development, our business development, and our organizational development in this rapidly evolving environment whose main characteristic is continuous change.

SOFTWARE DRIVES CHANGE

The rapidity of technological change is being driven by revolutions in information and communication (ICT) technologies. And underpinning ICT development is software engineering – the design and creation of code to control, coordinate, and run applications upon all the new computers, microprocessor devices, consumer electronics products, telephone and computer networks, digital cameras, MP3 players, e-books, mobile phones, and other ICT artifacts.

Developments in ICT – especially in software engineering – are, of course, catalyzing and accelerating developments in all other technology sectors (across the range from civil engineering to genetic research and biotechnology). As all these other sectors and domains of activity ''go digital'' so they also find that their activities are in transition from the atom business to the bit business. (Nicholas Negroponte of MIT describes the inevitable shift from atoms to bits in *Being Digital*.[1] He does not mean that we will stop manufacturing tangible products, more that the means of manufacturing – the robotics, automated machine tools, assembly plant – and the marketing and selling of these commodities will be mediated by bits, and that where tangibles (atoms) can be replaced by bits, they will be so replaced.) In other words, companies and organizations all around the world are increasingly finding that they are becoming *software* companies. It is happening to the music business right now; it's happening to the movie business; it's happening to the automobile business (and not only on the robotic production lines – the average new car has dozens of microprocessors and sensors collecting and processing data, running real-time diagnostics, and outputting information); it's already happened to the telecoms business, to financial services and banking, and, of course, to the videogame industry.

Software skills shortages

However, the realization in all these sectors of becoming a software-intensive operation poses issues long familiar to the ICT sector – notably that software engineers are a scarce commodity, and that productivity-gains in this area are a central management issue. This is no small matter. The demand for software exceeds our ability to provide it.

Recent studies by the Information Technology Association of America (April 2001) reveal the level of these shortages: 1 in 10 ICT jobs in the US are currently unfilled – over 850,000 jobs in this sector are vacant. Microsoft estimates that over the 12 months ending in April 2002 its business partners and customers will require 647,000 new IT professionals to support and develop business solutions on Microsoft products and technologies. These numbers reflect the IT workforce shortage in the US alone. Finding qualified workers is a global challenge. In the UK, WorkPermits UK lists a range of shortages encompassing not just software engineering, but firmware engineering and other related ICT skills shortages too.

Before these acute shortages, in the early days of computing, it was thought possible to speed up software engineering tasks by simply recruiting more staff, but this strategy had its problems too, as IBM and other software engineering organizations discovered as early as the 1960s and 1970s. Simply adding more programmers to the production cycle creates considerable coordination, training, and management problems – as well as being very expensive. In 1975, Frederick Brooks documented the experience of IBM in his book *The Mythical Man-month* – an account of the challenge faced by IBM in the creation of the operating system for their IBM360 mainframe.[2] Brooks came to the conclusion that adding extra personnel in an attempt to speed up the development process was not a viable solution, because of the escalating costs of training new team members, bringing them up to speed with developments, and in managing and coordinating their work.

So considerable efforts were made to improve software production methodologies and processes through the 1970s and 1980s, and considerable educational resources were devoted to building a pool of trained software engineers. However, there are still skill shortages in these sectors and, since the Web/Net is now truly global and provides the means to help resolve the problems that it is largely responsible for creating, developers have been looking farther afield to tap software skills around the world.

In the 1980s, as more rigorous software development methodologies were developed, and especially as tasks were partitioned more effectively at the architecture-design stage, and as the discipline of code documentation was enforced, so it became viable to add extra programmers as the software development cycle progressed. (Code documentation is the insertion of plain English comments and descriptions into the programming to clarify and describe otherwise hard-to-follow code.)

Modularized software development

As new programming languages emerged, and as software engineering evolved from a craft-based art to a routinized, industrial-strength operation, so it became possible to modularize tasks more efficiently, and therefore to outsource modules of programming. This rationalization of the software development process put much greater emphasis on the architectural design of the project – the innovation-intensive task of building a structure that embodies the conceptual solution produced as a result of defining and analyzing customer needs and requirements. The modularized tasks could be categorized at this stage, and the required programming work graded as to complexity and outsourced to the most suitable specialists, or to other teams in the same organization.

The search for cost-efficiencies in this process, and the growing availability of the enabling network connections and network bandwidth, led to the outsourcing of software engineering tasks – first to widely dispersed locations, then offshore, then to the idea that by outsourcing to developers on different Continents, it would be possible to build and sustain a global, 24-hour production cycle. Modules started in Japan could be handed on at the end of the working day to a team in Europe, then to a team in the US – optimizing the daily work patterns of programmers and fast-tracking the code production process. Costs could be cut by assigning routine programming or QA tasks to sites where wage costs were low, and more specialist tasks to sites with the appropriate expertise.

While this kind of process is made possible by falling telecommunications costs (and Internet use), and by increasing network bandwidth, it is only rarely exploited on a 24-hour basis, mainly due to the problems of coordination, monitoring, and managing such diurnal projects, but also to the fact that such rigorous, production-line processes mitigate against bottom-up innovation.

Innovation was seen as a process that took place at the interface between developer and client, generally in the main marketplace for software – the post-industrialized West. This led to a kind of software imperialism, with innovation focused in the West and routinized work parceled-out into countries where labor costs were low. The two results of this were that software engineers in the developing world were underutilized, and that the innovation engines in the West were still expensive. E-innovation is an emerging process for managing and encouraging innovation, and e-innovators are exploring several new responses to the software skills shortage, including processes that distribute and devolve the opportunity to innovate to individual developers and teams all around the world; and the exploitation of processes evolved by the open-source software development community (for more on these processes see Chapter 4, The E-Dimension). But e-innovation is more than this – it's a strategy for proactively responding to continuous change.

E-innovation

The current front-runner as a tool for accommodating and planning for change is the evolving process of e-innovation. E-innovation is the convergence of several previously rather separate disciplines and processes, bringing them together in a hybrid process that links technology scanning, technology forecasting, creativity, design, new product development, production, and marketing.

That this hasn't become formularized yet, or in any way formalized as a discipline, is what makes e-innovation such an interesting prospect. It's an area ripe for development and promises a *modus operandi* for proactively engaging with, and benefiting from, continuous change.

What we intend to present in this book is:

» a survey of the factors forcing us to engage in developing radical new ways of responding to change;
» the range of disciplines converging under the umbrella of e-innovation;
» its potential as a navigation tool for the discovery of new, profitable pathways through the ever-changing solution-space of the networked economy;
» the kind of principles and processes that will emerge; and
» how these principles and processes are currently being tested and trialed by some far-sighted businesses and corporations.

NOTES

1 Negroponte, Nicholas (1995) *Being Digital*. Alfred A. Knopf, New York.

2 Brooks, Frederick P. Jr (1975) *The Mythical Man-Month*. Addison-Wesley, Reading, MA.

The Evolution of E-Innovation

A short history of where e-innovation came from and how it reached this point. With:

» History of development
» History of recent web innovations
» Net new media timeline.

E-innovation processes began to emerge in the 1970s and 1980s, with the introduction of formal software design processes, and during the first wave of interactive multimedia product development, but e-innovation draws on disciplines that have emerged over the last 50 years of digital media history.

EMERGENCE OF E-INNOVATION

E-innovation is a new idea – a new label for a group of activities whose aim is to create new tools for innovation, product development and business development in the present climate of continuous change. These activities logically converge several previously separate but overlapping business processes including:

» *Competitive intelligence*
   technology scoping and research
   technology forecasting
   market intelligence
» *Strategic corporate planning*
   new business development
   planning new product development process
» *New product development*
   stage-gate process
   concept/idea generation
   design
   production planning
   software production
   marketing planning.

As there is considerable overlap between these activities, we can reduce the span of e-innovation to the three main headings: *competitive intelligence*, *strategic corporate planning*, and *new product development*, and in this section provide an overview of these areas and how they have evolved over the last 50 years or so.

COMPETITIVE INTELLIGENCE

No, this doesn't mean industrial espionage! Competitive intelligence (CI) is the collection, collation, and analysis of information from a wide variety of public sources such as trade shows, press releases, published corporate positioning and strategy documents, market research, industry or business sector surveys, reports and interviews, and articles and features in journals and magazines. Competitive intelligence professionals analyze this body of information on the activities of competitor businesses, their successes and failures in the marketplace, their aims, objectives and strategies. As the Society for Competitive Intelligence Professionals states: "Competitive Intelligence adds value to information gathering and strategic planning by introducing a disciplined system not only to gather information, but also to perform analysis and disseminate findings tailored to the needs of decision-makers" (from www.scip.org). Leonard M. Fuld, of competitive intelligence specialists Fuld & Company, describes competitive intelligence in ten key points:[1]

» information that has been analyzed to the point where you can make a decision;
» a tool to alert management to early warnings of both threats and opportunities;
» a means to deliver reasonable assessments; CI offers approximations and best views of the market and the competition;
» CI comes in many flavors (in technology intelligence, marketing intelligence, strategic intelligence, etc.);
» a way for companies to improve their bottom line;
» a way of life – a process – that becomes part and parcel of the normal operations of the entire organization, not just managers and CI professionals;
» CI is part of all best-in-class companies;
» CI is promoted from executive level throughout the organization;
» CI is seeing outside yourself – a corrective to the *not invented here* syndrome; and
» CI is both short and long term.

According to Prescott and Gibbons,[2] competitive intelligence is a program delivering "A formalized, yet continuously evolving process by which the management team assesses the evolution of its industry and the capabilities and behavior of its current and potential competitors to assist in maintaining or developing a competitive advantage." Of course, *the evolution of its industry* requires that we include technology scoping and forecasting and market intelligence under the general CI heading.

TECHNOLOGY SCOPING, RESEARCH AND ANALYSIS

This is variously called *environment scanning, technology intelligence, technology research and analysis*, and *technology scoping*. It is somewhat similar to the literature search – the first stage of academic research that involves locating and reading the extant literature on a particular topic. In a rapidly developing and changing technology landscape, useful sources of information on our dynamically changing environment are spread throughout the spectrum of media – in research journals, scientific papers, technical journals, R&D reports, management journals, etc. – and these are often aggregated on specialist websites (see Chapter 9 Key Concepts and Resources). The Web/Net also provides a range of other sources of technology intelligence, including access to the writings of many researchers, forecasters, and analysts; to the work and writings of experimental software designers, programmers, and cybernetic artists; to reports of work in development at university and corporate R&D centers, media labs, and computer science labs; to corporate annual reports, strategic-planning press releases, trader and market analyses; as well as to many thousands of Websites maintained by individual academics, researchers, and engineers. The task here is to scan or *scope* the technology environment, to develop a big picture of what is going on, and to identify the developments in technology that are important to your company, your marketplace, your products, and your plans. This can be done statistically – by listing occurrences of references to a particular technology, listing the occurrence of citations of a particular paper, listing search engine results on particular topics – and can be qualified by rating sources according to their verity and provenance.

TECHNOLOGY FORECASTING

Arising from technology research and the analysis of emerging technologies and identification of likely strands of development, technology forecasting uses a variety of techniques to create useful projections, and forecasts for particular development vectors likely to affect the development of a particular business, the implementation of a particular strategy, or the development of a particular product or group of products. The techniques used by the forecaster include:

» linear trend extrapolation
» searching for historical analogy
» canvassing experts (*Delphi* surveys)
» software modeling
» simulation and forecasting
» scenario-building.

With the growth of the Web/Net, the Delphi method of iteratively and regularly canvassing the opinion of experts in particular fields on particular subjects has become a realistic global exercise. For example the Department of Management Science at George Washington University (GWU) in Washington DC regularly publishes its *Forecast of Emerging Technologies: a continuous assessment of the technology revolution*, which is a Delphi survey of around 65 experts in different locations around the world, conducted largely through e-mail. But the Web is a valuable resource for trend forecasting in other ways too, with access to an abundance of news, information, and speculation on everything from new business models down to the underpinning R&D, and global standards specifications (and the rest) – it's all there if you know how to scope it and analyze it.

MARKET INTELLIGENCE

This includes a mix of statistical trend analysis (based on sales data and other results of market research), and lifestyle and fashion trend analysis and forecasting (mostly based on acute observation of current lifestyle trends). This latter art is widely used in the fashion and textiles industry to forecast fabrics, color, and style trends for coming seasons, and is based on couturier shows, mainstream fashion and textile shows, and the aggregated opinions of designers and lifestyle observers. There are several techniques deployed here, including the collection and collation of information on various trends as evidenced in demographic surveys, sales trends, and focus group research, and as witnessed by fashion and lifestyle magazines, specialist color- and fashion-forecasting agencies, UseNet discussion groups, and Websites (such as the discussion forums at www.trendsetting.org).

Designers use a number of techniques for short-term trend forecasting and design development, including the collection and collation of images and graphics into *concept boards* that show pictorial evidence of emerging trends (for example, in fashion clothing – identifying trends in color, cut, accessories, make-up, fabric, footwear, etc., or in product design – trends in styling, color finishes, manufacture, new materials, detailing, packaging, fabric/substrate finish, controlware, etc.).

Strategic corporate planning

There is no single generally accepted definition of strategic planning, but most people would agree that managing a large organization or corporation requires a long-range plan. Long-range planning is a three-step process:

» Analysis – of internal and external factors: internal strengths and weaknesses and external threats and opportunities, deriving from this exercise a definition of our distinctive competencies and key success factors.
» Vision – articulating the ideal to be aimed for.
» Direction – the development of alternatives and the evaluation of these alternatives, and the selection of a path to follow in pursuit of the vision.

This can involve the process of *gap analysis*. (Unless we are already a perfect organization, there will necessarily be a gap between our vision of the future and the reality of our present, and the analysis of this gap – in what ways our current organization differs from our ideal – is one of the primary tools of strategic planning. We need a good map if we are traveling through unfamiliar territory. Gap analysis compares the map of where we are now with the map of where we want to be, and indicates some of the ways in which we might marry the present with our desired future.

The idea of strategic planning has its roots in the military. *Webster's New World Dictionary* defines strategy as "the science of planning and directing large-scale military operations, of maneuvering forces into the most advantageous position prior to actual engagement with the enemy." But corporate strategic planning is a relatively new and still-evolving management art, and has a short and rather checkered history. First emerging in a wave of corporate enthusiasm in Eisenhower's USA, these early iterations appropriately reflected the traditional military planning model – an intensely vertical, top-down, hierarchical planning model in which the planning took place at senior executive level, typically involved a period of research, followed by time for analysis, consideration, and decision-making, then the publication of the plan. Interestingly, the *implementation* of the plan in these first experiments with corporate planning was typically considered as a separate operation, quite distinct from the conceptual stage.

The 1950s strategic planning process rested heavily on SWOT analysis (the assessment of a company's strengths, and weaknesses, and the opportunities and threats it faced). From the 1960s to the 1990s, various planning models enjoyed periods of success, and the strategic planning options expanded to include qualitative and quantitative modeling, the shareholder-value model, the Porter model (the "five forces" model of competitive structure); life-cycle analysis (tracking our products against the cycle of introduction, growth, maturity and decline); product portfolio analysis, industry attractiveness-business strength model; the business transformation model, and other models. And as strategic planning models were developed and refined to cope with the demands of planning in environments of constant change, so they came to deploy the multivariate "matrix" schematics to model the complex relationships of external and internal factors, product cycles and portfolio management. These matrix models are, like most multivariate problems (i.e., those with many contributory factors to consider), best handled by computer. Recently there have been several strategic planning tools and executive support system (ESS) tools developed, notably the IBM Business Systems Planning and Information Quality Analysis, and Andersen Consulting's Strategic Information Planning, but these programs have been criticized as expensive to implement and too rigid (with a limited ability to learn and adapt in response to rapid change). However, there is considerable scope for development in this area. AI (the field of artificial intelligence) has already developed several techniques that could extend these kind of expert-system approaches to include the ability to learn, assess, and adapt to change. Much e-innovation is taking place in this area, from the development of established corporate strategy tools like SAP AG's Enterprise Resource Planning software, and, for example, Powersim's Business Planning Simulation tools, which are based on the Systems Dynamics model created by systems pioneer Jay Forrester in the 1960s. Some of the possible developments here include the use of AI tools such as neural networks, fuzzy logic, software agents, and machine-learning. Importantly, these directions promise to integrate planning, implementation, and changing conditions into adaptive and evolving programs deploying extensive feedback loops.

STAGE-GATE PROCESS

Planning for innovation and creating adaptive and responsive processes for new product development (NPD) resulted in the emergence of monitoring and checking procedures that aimed at reducing risk and exposure in NPD. The stage-gate process is one such method. Now in use in some of the world's biggest businesses (Proctor & Gamble, Du Pont, Exxon), stage-gate has many devotees, including Paul Belliveau, president of the International Product Development and Management Association. It involves five main stages or gates through which the new product has to pass during development. The product has to meet rigid criteria to pass through a gate and proceed to the next stage. According to one of the developers of stage-gate, Robert G. Cooper[3] of Ontario's McMaster University, a "gatekeeper" or review panel assesses the development through these five stages:

1 preliminary investigation – the assessment of technology solution, proposed market and projected costs;
2 detailed investigation – the stage of building the business case, defining customer or user needs and wants, providing detailed market analysis, concept testing and thorough technical assessment;
3 product development – including lead-customer or user-group testing and monitoring, and development of a marketing and production plan;
4 testing and validation – test-marketing, full customer/user testing, and trial production; and

5 full production and market launch – implementation of production and marketing plans, and mechanism for continual monitoring and product development.

NEW BUSINESS DEVELOPMENT

The kind of analysis that results from the overlapping activities of competitive intelligence, technology scoping and research, technology forecasting, market intelligence, and strategic corporate planning – sometimes called strategic new product development – helps planners identify product development opportunities for extending and/or adapting existing product lines and business models, for the development of new products and for the exploration of new routes to market and new business opportunities.

The realization that these new business models might emerge from the bottom up is one of the products of the kind of *network effect* analysis that impacted on our thinking in the 1990s. The insights of Kevin Kelly (*Out of Control*)[4] and James Moore (''business ecosystems''),[5] based in part on revisiting postwar systems theory, and games, ecology and cybernetic theories and thinking, forced a radical reappraisal of how innovation occurs in a massively networked environment, and how businesses might adapt to these network effects.

New product development

New product development (NPD) is the process of creating new products and bringing them to market. Here *new* usually means *new to the producer*, and may be a product that the producer has not made or marketed before, significant updates to a product already made by the producers, or rarely, a product wholly new to the marketplace, defining a new sector of commerce or genre of product. Strategic new product development is the link between NPD and corporate strategic planning; it is the establishment of NPD deep in the thinking and guidance of the company, and seeks to establish a close harmony between strategic planning and day-to-day tactical operations. Strategic new product development encompasses many of the processes of e-innovation, but e-innovation is more appropriate to NPD in the software and ICT sectors, and is providing new insights and processes for new product development in other sectors.

The NPD process involves several of the e-innovation stages already outlined, including competitive intelligence and strategic corporate planning, and generally follows a common basic pattern of activities, often using a stage-gate approach:

» *environment scoping* – technology forecasting and other forms of competitive intelligence, pointing to possible NPD opportunities;
» *opportunity mapping* – the identification and initial exploration of possible NPD opportunities;
» *conceptual structuring* – the creation of a concept statement or document summarizing product ideas, potential or actual customers, and financial projections;
» *project initiation* – the launch of the development project, building of development team, partners and test-customer base;
» *prototype* – the rapid prototyping of the product or at least some of the key features within the product – enough to give test customers a useable product test bed;
» *initial exposure* – the testing of new product with partners and test customers;
» *complete development* – the complete build of the project to internal (alpha) test stage; and
» *test implementation* – the final phase before full product commercialization, involves launching and testing with a wider group of customers.

DESIGN

Design has many definitions, both as a noun and a verb. Here we will define it as the process by which product ideas are given form. Designers from different sectors employ different approaches to design, but here we are going to use a process model typical of the multimedia software design sector – the model most appropriate to web design. This process includes:

» *creating the brief* – the aims and objectives of the project and any constraints – the brief is the co-creation of both client and developer;
» *mapping solution space* – integrating competitive intelligence, technology scoping, etc.;

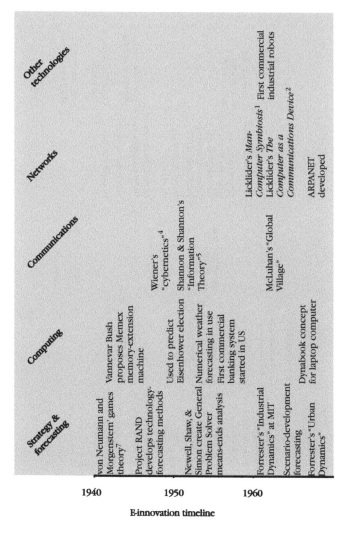

Strategy & forecasting	Computing	Communications	Networks	Other technologies
von Neumann and Morgenstern' games theory[7]				
Project RAND develops technology-forecasting methods	Vannevar Bush proposes Memex memory-extension machine			
	Used to predict Eisenhower election	Wiener's "cybernetics"[4]		
Newell, Shaw, & Simon create General Problem Solver means-ends analysis	Numerical weather forecasting in use First commercial banking system started in US	Shannon & Shannon's "Information Theory"[5]		
Forrester's "Industrial Dynamics" at MIT		McLuhan's "Global Village"	Licklider's Man-Computer Symbiosis[1] Licklider's The Computer as a Communications Device[2]	First commercial industrial robots[2]
Scenario-development forecasting				
Forrester's "Urban Dynamics"	Dynabook concept for laptop computer		ARPANET developed	

1940   1950   1960

E-innovation timeline

Fig. 3.1 E-innovation timeline.

Forrester's "World Dynamics" used by Club of Rome for forecasting	Microsoft founded		ARPANET e-mail invented	
Porter's strategic information system thinking "Forces Driving Industry Competition"	First spreadsheet First commercial word processor		Turoff's *The Network Nation*[3] MINITEL launched	ATMs introduced Compact disc technology announced
Pask's *Microman*[8]	IBM introduce PC Lotus 1-2-3 released 6M computers sold		Tim Berners Lee proposes World Wide Web networked hypertext system, HTML and HTTP	
Axelrod's "Evolution of Cooperation"[9]	"Copyleft" used by hacker Don Hopkins GNU Manifesto for a "free" operating system	Live digital radio broadcast	World Wide Web introduced	
Senge's "Fifth Discipline"[10]				
Schwartz's *The Art of the Long View*[11]	Linux released as free software	ISDN lines for commercial use	Mosaic web browser 16.5mn Usenet users	DVD consumer players launched
Brandenburger & Nalebuff's "Coopetition"[12]			Amazon.com started Hotmail started	Commercial use of smartcards
Kogut & Turcanu: "emergence of e-innovation"[13]		Japan's DoCoMo I-Mode service has 7mn users		Sony robot dog AIBO introduced
1980	**1990**	**2000**		

E-innovation timeline

Fig. 3.1 *(Continued)*.

» *divergent ideas* – the rapid production of many ideas appropriate to the brief;

» *convergent propositions* – the choice of the most appropriate solution(s) and the presentation of these ideas to the client as visuals, flowcharts, and written treatments;

» *production planning* – team building, recruitment of specialists, asset (contents) scoping, specifications and design briefs for programmers and designers, scheduling, budgeting, etc.

» *demonstration prototype* – the creation of a working interactive model of the project, with indicative graphic styling and navigation, but with dummy contents – for presentation to client – to clearly illustrate functioning and intended style to development team and sometimes for preliminary testing with focus group;

» *program build* – includes specialist tasks such as:
  » asset sourcing and digital formatting;
  » content editorial and information architecture design;
  » program architecture;
  » interface and navigation design;
  » content design and graphic template design;
  » specialist design – animation, Flash, 3D, VR, audio, etc.;
  » specialist programming – databases, VRML, XML, Java applets, etc.; and
  » quality assurance and testing.

» *alpha testing* – internal testing, user testing and debugging;

» *beta testing* – "soft release" of product to limited customer base for testing and feedback; and

» *general release* – launch of product to the market.

TIMELINE

Timeline notes

Networks

1 Licklider described the potential of shared conceptual models accessed by multiple users of computer systems. Licklider, Joseph (1960) *Man-Computer Symbiosis* at http://www.memex.org/licklider.html

2 On the eve of ARPANET, Licklider's masterful thesis on the power of networked computing envisions human brains working with machine intelligence to create "a partnership that will think as no human being has ever thought." Licklider, Joseph, and Taylor, Robert (1968) *The Computer as a Communications Device* at http://www.memex.org/licklider.html

3 Turoff, Murray (1993) *The Network Nation* (first published 1978). MIT Press, Cambridge, MA.

Communications

4 Wiener, Norbert (1948) *Cybernetics, or Control and Communication in the Animal and the Machine*. MIT Press, Cambridge, MA.

5 Shannon, Claude E. and Weaver, Warren (1949) *The Mathematical Theory of Communication*. University of Illinois Press, Urbana, IL – introduces Information Theory

6 McLuhan, Marshal (1964) *Understanding Media*. Routledge and Kegan Paul, London – coins the term 'Global Village'

Strategy and forecasting techniques

7 Neumann, John von and Morgenstern, Oskar (1944) *Theory of Games and Economic Behavior*. Princeton University Press, Princeton, NJ.

8 Pask, Gordon with Curran, Susan (1982) *Microman*. Century Publishing, London – popularizes cybernetics

9 Axelrod, Robert (1984) *The Evolution of Cooperation*. Basic Books, New York.

10 Senge, Peter (1990) *The Fifth Discipline*. Doubleday, New York.

11 Schwartz, Peter (1996) *The Art of the Long View – planning for the future in an uncertain world*. Doubleday, New York.

12 Brandenburger, Adam M. and Nalebuff, Barry J. (1996) *Coopetition: 1 A Revolutionary Mindset that redefines competition and cooperation; 2: The Game Theory strategy that's changing the game of business*. Doubleday, New York.

13 Kogut, Bruce and Turcanu, Anca (1999) *Global software development and the emergence of e-innovation* at http://cbi.gsia.cmu.edu/new-web/1999SFconference/Kogut/Kogut.html

NOTES

1 Fuld, Leonard (1995) *The New Competitive Intelligence.* John Wiley & Sons, New York, and at www.fuld.com

2 Prescott, John E. and Gibbons, Patrick T. (1993). "Global Competitive Intelligence: An Overview" in J.E. Prescott and P.T. Gibbons (eds) *Global Perspectives on Competitive Intelligence.* Society of Competitive Intelligence Professionals, Alexandria, VA.

3 Cooper, Robert G. (1993) *Winning at New Products.* Addison-Wesley, Reading, MA.

4 Kelly, Kevin (1994) *Out of Control: The New Biology of Machines.* Fourth Estate, London.

5 Moore, James F. (1999) *The Death of Competition: Leadership and Strategy in the Age of Business Ecosystems.* Harper Business, New York.

The E-Dimension:

E-Innovation

- » All companies are software companies
- » Global sourcing
- » Outsourcing innovation
- » E-innovation: outsourcing and open sourcing
- » Open sourcing.

Does continuous change demand continuous innovation? And how do you plan that continuous innovation in your products, your services and your business?

The last 20 years have been characterized by the trickle down of microprocessor power from personal computers through to videogame consoles, to consumer electronics, to white goods, to phones, even to the Tamagotchi toys that you clip on your key ring. This product of Moore's Law[1] and mass production has catalyzed a constant stream of innovation in computing, in telecommunications, and in the way we interface with media. And it doesn't stop there. The destiny of all our manufactured goods – from the factories which make things, to the vehicles we drive, to the clothes we wear, and even to the food we eat – is bound up with the microprocessor. We have chips in fridges, chips in food packaging, chips in credit cards, chips in birthday and Christmas cards, food with chips or with machine-readable labeling, microprocessors woven into our clothes, chips doubling as jewelry, chips monitoring our health and our environment, chip cameras, chip records, chip books, even chip pens that digitally record everything we write or draw with them. The microprocessor is destined to become ever more omnipresent in our lives.

What's more, these chips will be talking to each other – and sometimes to us humans too! They will expedite communications between machines and between people, providing evermore sophisticated voice recognition, speech synthesis, multimedia communications tools, multi-party workware and socialware – even automatic language translation. Chips will interface cyberspace and the real world in all kinds of ways that we can now only guess at – in surveillance, environmental monitoring, biometrics (checking our pulse, blood pressure and other key health indicators), in traffic control, and much more besides. And what drives microprocessors is *software*.

ALL COMPANIES ARE SOFTWARE COMPANIES

Where there's a chip, there's software. Software drives processes at every level of our deeply intertwined economy: from international currency exchanges and stock exchanges to personal organizers and e-mail. And neither is it just in the ICT sector. Software drives our economy through all sectors; financial services went digital first, then entertainment (the music business has been digital since the early 1980s), Hollywood is increasingly digital, publishing is digital, TV is digital – and digital means *software*. Travel, retail, manufacturing, governance, health, law and policing, shipping, transport – every industry is increasingly reliant on software. And the Information Technology Association of America reports (April 2001) that non-IT companies are by far the larger employers of IT workers in the US. The way companies develop and innovate in software is becoming a key driver of success.

This is the process that Media Labs' Nicholas Negroponte calls "the transition from atoms to bits." The change in emphasis from physical artifacts to informational artifacts in our newly emerging digital economy is inevitable and exponential: from the CD disk to the MP3 file, from the book to the e-book text, from paper to screen, from cash to digital cash, we are busy dematerializing our cultural economy into software, and this process is accelerating, as Negroponte points out:

"The change from atoms to bits is irrevocable and unstoppable. Why now? Because the change is also exponential – small differences today have suddenly shocking consequences tomorrow."

Nicholas Negroponte (1995)[2]

We are all involved in this change. We are all corporately and personally affected by this transition. Our buying habits, the artifacts we acquire, how we manage our money, how we telecommunicate, what we watch, listen to and read, how we take photos, make videos, record music, get news, find information – all these processes are increasingly *software* processes or are increasingly mediated or driven by software.

The switch from atoms to bits has major implications for business. As every company perforce becomes a software company, and the demand for software increases, the search for more efficient software-production strategies, and for increased productivity gains in the labor-intensive software engineering process, becomes increasingly important. For the last few decades the demand for software engineers has exceeded supply in all advanced postindustrial countries.

Bruce Kogut and Anca Meitu of Pennsylvania University's Wharton School argue, in a recent important paper, that there are two main models for coping with this increased demand. Fundamental to both models is the Web/Net itself – the ability of software engineers all around the world to participate and cooperate in the creation of new software. (See Chapter 9, Key Concepts and Resources.)

> "Quite simply, the Net has the potential to make the research labs of industrial firms look insular and antiquated. And it has the potential to introduce a fundamentally new research model since the founding of internal research labs at the beginning of the (last) century."
>
> *Bruce Kogut and Anca Meitu (2000)[3]*

Global sourcing

Kogut and Meitu's first model is that of global sourcing – the dominant current strategy – growing logically from local outsourcing or "satellite" software production (modularizing a software task and farming-out this work to several development teams). This relatively new ability to source software from engineers and software engineering companies all around the world means that (a) the more routine programming tasks can be sourced from countries where labor costs are lower, (b) modules can be placed according to the particular expertise of the outsource teams, and (c) that by exploiting time differences around the world, continuous 24-hour (diurnal) cycles of software development become possible.

Global outsourcing like this depends rather heavily on the efficacy of the initial software design or "architectural" planning (how the program is constructed and then designed to be modularized for independent development). And it demands considerable centralized management, and excellent (preferably broadband) communications for the coordination of often widely dispersed teams. (Broadband connections allow more than just fast data communications between remote sites. They also allow synchronous voice and videoconferencing, web conferencing, shared digital whiteboards, and other multiparty collaborative groupware to enhance technical briefings, coordination, and communication between teams at different locations.

The idea of a global, 24-hour software "factory", where blocks of code are developed in one time zone and electronically passed on at the end of a working day to another time zone further west, promised massive gains from lower costs and shorter production times. But as Kogut and Meitu point out, this kind of "diurnal development" depends heavily on centralized planning and coordination, and reinforces the notion that the initial innovation (design and new product planning) is also centralized – mostly in the leading postindustrial nations.

Outsourcing innovation

Innovation occurs most frequently at the interface between the software designer and the customer. It is often the case that innovative software solutions are created as the programmer or systems analyst deconstructs the customer's problem or objective and proposes various solutions. Often customers' needs will drive innovation. Solutions can be proposed and the chosen solution or solutions can then be specified and planned for modular construction (a process much facilitated by object-oriented software development tools, and languages like C++ and Java). That this initial innovation is often the result of close collaboration with clients and customers means that the off-shore software developers and engineers are delegated the more routine tasks of coding. While this can be cost-effective (parceling out really routine tasks to countries where labor is cheap), the diurnal production line does little to encourage local or bottom-up innovation, evolution, or improvement because it is difficult to accommodate the bottom-up problem solving and insights of globally dispersed (but often equally capable) software engineers straitjacketed into a product-line solution proposed back at the client interface.

E-innovation: outsourcing and open sourcing

What Kogut and Meitu propose as their second model switches the emphasis from this "imperialistic" model of centralized innovation to accommodate what they rightly identify as the most important impact of the Web/Net – the bottom-up innovation potential promised by "the increase in the number of innovators stirring the witches brew [of the Web] on a global basis."

This happens in two main ways: first the logical step of outsourcing innovation – cutting out the often expensive Western software innovation company and taking your problems and objectives direct to one of the many software suppliers based in India, Russia, or Eastern Europe. Software is a global industry, and software innovation is not confined just to those countries that have the main markets. The proximity of customers to software innovators is no longer a key condition of innovation. Design and technical briefings can be made through the Web/Net. Solutions can be delivered the same way. The customer might never meet the software engineer.

Alternatively, a large software company can set up satellite operations offshore – utilizing lower-cost labor while still keeping software design and innovation in-house, or encourage bottom-up innovation by "componentizing" software. Much as Netscape, Adobe, Quark and other software houses encouraged developers to build extensions, plug-ins and software modules for their products by releasing software development tools, tutorials, and shareware. Palm – the market-leader in handheld computers – has created a global network of over 3,500 software engineering companies and individuals developing programs, applications, and tools for their PalmPilot and other personal digital assistants (PDAs), thereby encouraging a continuous stream of innovation to enhance their products.

The market-leaders in videogame consoles realized very early the importance of building developer networks to create and supply the games for their systems. The larger the pool of developers, the greater the chance of a hit product. The publishing industry and record business have of course operated in much the same way, relying on external composers, performers, and writers to generate a sufficiently large pool of products that might generate best-sellers, chart-toppers, and must-have products.

Open sourcing

Secondly, Kogut and Meitu point to another way of harnessing the "Net effect" of bottom-up innovation: the revolutionary impact of open-source development. In this radical shift away from purely proprietary coding, a company or individual releases not just development tools and software libraries for modularized developments of plug-ins and extensions, but the actual source code of their program (an operating system, browser, application, or whatever), publishing it "freely" on the Web/Net, just as Netscape released the source code for Communicator 5.0 in 1998 in a considered attempt to stay ahead of Microsoft in the race to develop their web-browsing products. Kogut and Meitu argue: "Open source development is a process that enables innovations in software to be accomplished in a distributed community."

However, this innovation strategy applies equally to hardware development. The global success of the IBM-originated Personal Computer (the PC) over proprietary computer architectures like the Apple Macintosh (and the Atari computer, and others) is commonly ascribed to the fact that the PC is "open architecture" – i.e., it could be assembled from parts manufactured by many hundreds (perhaps thousands) of component makers. This encouraged bottom-up innovation, lined the pockets of the operating system and GUI-software suppliers (Microsoft owned MS-DOS and Windows), and built Intel into a dominant microprocessor company. This is a classic example of what James Moore calls *coopetition* – the cooperation of many independent companies in the creation of a market in which they can then compete for market share. What's more, as Kogut and Meitu point out, software engineering is a "laboratory" for studying how innovation can be planned for other industries.

The advantages of open source are that there is a huge pool of web-connected programmers, hackers, and other software engineers in the world. They are deeply conscious of the Web/Net traditions of shared software, free advice and opinion in newsgroups, the value of free exchange of ideas through chat forums, bulletin boards, e-mail and other web communications media. They constitute an expert workforce much, much larger than any single company could employ. This culture of shareware is embodied for the OSS (open-source software) community in the GNU public license (GPL for short), which legally helps protect open-source software from exploitation or privatization by individuals or companies. OSS is the "triumph of the commons", and GNU's copyright is called *copyleft*.

Apart from the tradition of sharing and cooperation, what else motivates individual software engineers to devote time and talent to the solution of OSS programming problems and refinements? Kogut and Meitu point to three main reasons:

1 *Reciprocity*. An unpublished paper by Eric von Hippel, entitled "Emerging economies of virtual communities: 'Free' user-to-user

assistance in open-source communities" (unpublished paper, MIT) documents the importance of reciprocity in the support groups for Apache – one of the leading server-software applications (and one of the great successes of the open-source movement). Here, the most important reason why individuals posted answers on Usenet groups is the desire to help, because they in turn have been helped by others, or because they expect to benefit from this kind of free advice, assistance and help in future.

2 *Professional status.* Working on proprietary software is by definition a private, internal company project, and programmers are often completely anonymous. By participating in OSS development, the programmer effectively publishes his or her work for the scrutiny and appraisal of their peers – it's a form of publishing, akin to getting your science paper published in a major journal or review, and it looks great on the CV – and, more importantly, gets commented upon, referred to and talked about in the developer community.

In my own experience of working closely with software developers, there is a passionate attachment to, even an idealistic nostalgia for, a golden age of cooperation and mutual aid, in their attitude to OSS. Linus Torvalds (the creator and guiding mentor of Linux, the OSS version of Unix) whose Linux operating system is one of the other great and evolving triumphs of the OSS movement, is held in awe. Likewise Bill Joy, who as CTO of Sun Microsystems, helped create Java, a programming language that enjoys huge OSS support. The community of developers welcomes gurus and amateur programmers alike. Got a problem? "Post it and get it fixed" is a solution resorted to by the overwhelming majority of developers. Posting a query through a news group or other Web/Net online service invariably calls forth generous responses from the global software community. Of course, for an OSS project to work, it must be of intrinsic interest to the developer community. It must also be seen that acceptance of a contribution confers prestige upon the contributor.

3 *Remuneration.* Although contributions to OSS development are made freely, without condition, often the prestige of working on an OSS development is reflected either in the ability to attract a higher salary (being an accepted part of the Linux developer community commands a $10k salary premium, according to hearsay). And it's

not just salaries, new forms of remittance for software developers include royalties instead of, or as well as, fees and stock options in the organization *productivizing* the OSS project (i.e., as Red Hat productivizes Linux).

How the methods of open-source software development, global sourcing, and the other more centrally-directed methods of conventional new product development might be integrated or co-evolved into a viable e-innovation strategy we'll investigate in Chapter 5, The Global Dimension.

RED HAT: HOW TO SELL FREE SOFTWARE

In 1991 a young Finnish hacker called Linus (pronounced *Lee-nus*) Torvalds posted a message on an Internet newsgroup forum devoted to minix developers (comp.os.minix – minix is a compact version of Unix), announcing that he was developing, as a hobby, a free operating system for PCs. (*Free* in those days was used in the same way that open source is used now.) This Unix-like software became known as Linux, and Torvalds proved to be not only a great programmer, but an accomplished evangelizer, guru and central linchpin of the open-source movement.

Linux became one of the prime examples of the success of open-source development – a process characterized by multiple independent developers collaborating through the Internet and working for free to develop brilliantly robust and effective software solutions that are not "owned" by anybody. Open source is a "triumph of the commons." The *free* means that Linux is freely available for any software developer or user to copy and use – and to update, amend, or tweak, as long as these amendments are freely distributed too. Every Linux user benefits from the collaborative and solitary efforts of every other Linux user. Linux, like Unix is a very modular operating system. Open source processes mean that specialist software (drivers for particular bits of hardware, for example) developed for a particular organization, then become freely available to anyone else who needs them. By 2001 there were approximately 17 million Linux users (http://counter.li.org).

But while Linux is great software, and appeals hugely to the developer community (for some of the reasons outlined in Chapter 4, The E-dimension), it was not a consumer-friendly product – you couldn't buy it in a box with a printed manual and simple installation instructions – nor was there a central source of help and support. Sure, you could go "newsgrouping" and seek help from the open-source community, but there was no central distributor that an individual, ordinary (non-specialist) user or organization could turn to. It wasn't an easy enterprise package. That's why, in 1993, a small group of developers in North Carolina decided to make it easier for people to access and to try. Their approach was to become a model for open-source distribution. Unlike other OSS distribution sources, they developed a package method of distributing Linux. Users could buy a package of fully tested and configured Linux software that was ready to install and run – and importantly, could be just as easily un-installed, without affecting the version you already had. The North Carolina group, headed by Marc Ewing, were joined by Bob Young, an entrepreneurial reseller of Linux systems, and together they created Red Hat during 1994-5.

Linux is free. But before Red Hat came along, customers had to be IT experts – they had to select items they wanted from several hundred different options, download several (often several dozen) pieces of software, configure and install them. Now this didn't stop people adopting Linux, it was free after all, and it was well proven, customizable, and had a world-wide developer network supporting it – but it wasn't *easy*. There was another issue retarding the growth of the Linux market – the reluctance of IT managers in larger businesses to adopt software that had no clear and contactable point of presence – no provenance, as it were. Did you really want to tell the boss you got the company's core enterprise software from a bunch of teenage hackers? That it was developed by a global, non-profit making, libertarian cooperative?

Red Hat came into this marketplace with the notion that it was possible to make money by *selling* free software. Bob Young has said that it's no more difficult selling *free* software than it is selling proprietary software – you build a great product, market it brilliantly, look after your customers, and thereby build a quality brand.

> "Marketing with skill and imagination, particularly in highly competitive markets, requires that you offer solutions to your customers that others cannot or will not match. To that end open-source – where the actual source-code of the software is freely available, and re-distributable – is not a liability but a competitive advantage. The open-source development model produces software that is stable, flexible and highly customisable. So the vendor of open-source software starts with a quality product. The trick is to devise an effective way to make money delivering the benefits of open-source software to your clients."
>
> *Robert Young (1999)[4]*

What Red Hat did was to (a) provide the provenance and point of contact, and (b) collect, collate, test, certify and package Linux into a set of 435 separate packages, and make it easy for customers to buy, install, configure and customize their software. The Red Hat distribution method makes Linux easier to install and maintain. It provides users with simple point and click installation and system administration tools, all based on this package idea. Developed by Marc Ewing, the package distribution method came to be called the Red Hat Package Manager (RPM).

Red Hat's innovation of adding value to free software is very successful, they were capitalized at over $19bn in the tech-stock boom of 1999, and are still (2001) worth a respectable £1bn. And their success has inspired other companies to move into this opportunity space between free open-source and paying customers. In 2000, Great Bridge (www.greatbridge.com), a privately funded company based in Norfolk, Virginia, started packaging PostgreSQL, a popular and powerful open-source database. Great Bridge will promote, market and provide professional support services for PostgreSQL in much the same way that Red Hat does for Linux.

NOTES

1 Moore's Law: the observation by Gordon Moore in 1966 that integrated circuits (later microprocessors) doubled in capacity every 18 months, for the same relative cost.

2 Negroponte, Nicholas (1995) *Being Digital*. Alfred A. Knopf, New York.

3 Kogut, Bruce and Meitu, Anca (2000) *The Emergence of E-innovation: Insights from Open-Source Software Development* (working paper of the Reginald F. Jones Center, The Wharton School). University of Pennsylvania, PA.

4 Young, Robert (1999) "How Red Hat Software stumbled across a new economic model and helped improve an industry" in *Open Sources: Voices from the Open Source Revolution*. O'Reilly and Associates, Cambridge, MA.

The Global Dimension

The global dimension – implications of globalization and issues raised.

- » A strategy for winning
- » Opensource and big business
- » Cambridge Interactive and open source
- » Open-source success
- » Public/private development
- » Outsourcing and open sourcing.

E-innovation is the emerging art of harnessing the bottom-up power of globally networked individuals and teams to conceive better products, and to create them and bring them to market more efficiently, through a combination of internal design, planning and new product development methodologies and global innovation-sourcing and open sourcing (open-source software development).

E-innovation has implications far beyond the software sector, though as we have pointed out (in Chapter 4, The E-dimension), the software sector actually pervades almost every aspect of our economy and our culture. (Most companies are now software companies to some greater or lesser degree.) E-innovation methodologies can be applied to other manufacturing and service sectors. In a section (entitled "A Wider Speculation") of their recent paper, Bruce Kogut and Anca Meitu suggest:

> "E-innovation is not just possible for software, but for all fields in which cooperation can be arranged by modules and [in which there exists] a wide understanding of a common language and culture."
>
> *Bruce Kogut and Anca Meitu (2000)[1]*

A STRATEGY FOR WINNING

E-innovation promises competitive advantage for businesses around the world, and across many sectors of the economy. It might be the most efficacious proactive corporate response to the pressures of continuous changes in technology, in business development and in the marketplace. It is also, notably, a network-based response to the rapid changes catalyzed by the (inter) network itself – in this light, e-innovation can be regarded as an emergent quality of massively networked individuals, teams, and corporations. It's emerging as a strategy for winning in the twenty-first century real-time business ecosystem.

A key to the successful development of e-innovation methods for a particular business lies in the integration of the iterative processes of design and planning with problem solving and the creation of architectural structures for product development that can be modularized and segmented for global outsourcing or open sourcing.

Open source and big business

For example, initially we'll look at how IBM became the first Fortune 100 company to become a full member of the open-source community, then focus briefly on how a smaller software developer uses OSS development techniques in the creation and maintenance of its proprietary software products.

During the mid-1990s, IBM development teams, spearheaded by project manager Dave Shields, developed an extremely fast Java source-to-bytecode compiler – nicknamed *Jikes* – and in 1997 released the Jikes compiler in binary form for open-source development. Jikes takes programming code written in Java and compiles it into code that runs on the Java Virtual Machine (JVM) – the software computer that is built into many browsers, many access devices, PDAs, PCs etc., and allows Java to run on anything that can run a JVM – and it does this extremely fast. Jikes for Linux was released in July 1998, and the response was gratifying; over 15,000 copies were downloaded in the first three months after the release – more downloads in 3 months than in the previous 15 months. For Java developers, Jikes had several advantages over other compilers: it was strictly Java-compatible (rigorously adhering to both Java language and JVM specifications), it was open source, certified by the Open-Source Initiative, and it was a high performance product, ideal for use with large-scale projects.

IBM has shown great faith in the OSS community and has committed considerable resources to the open-source projects it runs (of which Jikes was one of the earliest). Why should a hard-nosed business like IBM get involved in radical developer communities like this? Simply because the potential of OSS development is enormous – a large pool of independent developers, typically driven by the factors we described in Chapter 4, The E-dimension, with their coding contributions freely given for assessment and appraisal by their peers – and no company should ignore the opportunity to explore how best they can work with or learn from the OSS developer community.

What were IBM's motives in releasing Jikes? According to the background feature on the Jikes home page (http://oss.software.ibm.com), the release of Jikes was a visible demonstration of IBM's commitment to open standards and to Java; it was the optimum way to make Jikes more accessible and more reliable, it encouraged more widespread use of Java, and the adherence to Java standards, and importantly – it gave IBM some experience of actually running an open-source project.

CAMBRIDGE INTERACTIVE AND OPEN SOURCE

Another example of how commercial software developers are adopting OSS development strategies is cited by Jeanna Murray at IBM's DeveloperWorks. Cambridge Interactive (CI; an Internet and online services company) have adopted some OSS development techniques to accelerate the development of their proprietary software products. Although the design of the program architecture and project planning is still the job of an individual or small team, OSS techniques enable CI to accelerate the processes of prototyping, coding, and debugging new features.

Murray quotes CI's CEO Andy Singleton: ''The development process really is distributed, and it really is scaleable in a way that even the largest commercial software projects rarely achieve,'' he says. ''This is because every developer has all of the source code and at least local permission to modify it. There are fewer barriers to fixing a bug or fixing an entire architecture.'' He further points out that the removal of these barriers, removes ''a web of dependencies'' that inevitably causes delay in conventional software development programs.

Cambridge Interactive compensates for what Singleton sees as typical open-source weaknesses by creating a traditional development infrastructure, based on the initial architecture process as well as documentation and packaging. What CI are doing is *utilizing OSS development methods to streamline their software development process*. They distribute their code under strict copyright license to their distributed team of developers, customers and partners. Of course the development team need a common platform accessible to all. For CI these include C, C++, Perl and Java.

Open-source developers use standard e-mail and mailing lists to communicate, and keep tabs on developments in their project by means of a Website that provides access to the latest releases, source code, development tools, code libraries, and a bug-tracking database. Commercial developers opt for a higher degree of security, often preferring commercial groupware for collaborative work. CI uses its own software, a development process-management application called

Power Steering, which enables managers to set up project team members, discussion groups and shared documentation areas, and control *permissioning* – the sign-off acceptance of updates to the core program. All members of the team can register for alerts that indicate new items, documents, postings or discussion topics of special interest to them. Power Steering also provides tools for the hierarchical breakdown of projects, tasking, and reporting. Instead of open-source tools like CVS (Current Versions System) to manage source code, CI use Microsoft's Visual SourceSafe and Source Offsite, which provides secure, encrypted authentication and communication facilities.

PUBLIC/PRIVATE DEVELOPMENT

The wider potential of this kind of public/private software development is easy to see. It is in the creation of tools (and even whole development teams) that provide the interface between OSS and proprietary development. These may be tools like Power Steering, or other packages that offer distributed development environments with integrated communications and source management, such as SourceForge and Open Avenue. Currently these environments are simply aggregations of standard Internet tools aimed primarily at open-source developers, but CI's Singleton expects them to offer support for proprietary developers too. There are also sites that match developers to projects, like www.guru.com, www.iNiku.com, and www.freeagent.com, which focus on matching individual developers to projects, and www.ITSquare.com, which matches your project to development companies who will pitch and quote for the work.

Of course, it is entirely logical that new networking opportunities and new software development and collaborative tools should affect how software is developed in this globally networked community of programmers and engineers. Jeanne Murray quotes Andy Singleton's "rules of the road" for new software development strategies extensively at http://oss.software.ibm.com, but I'll just summarize them here:

» *Early design should fit on a napkin.* The software architecture in open-source style distributed developments is very important and the description of data structures and modules should be simple and short.

» *Take time to research standards and tools.* The productivity of the distributed team depends on the right tools. These are developing continuously, and research necessarily takes time, but adequate time spent scoping, identifying and choosing tools will reap benefits in productivity throughout the project.

» *Start with something that works* – an initial prototype or "build 0" – a minimum version of the software that can be assembled and tested.

» *Build incrementally.* Building and testing software requires the resources of people and equipment and is facilitated by automatic processes. To be scaleable for OSS-style distributed development, the build schedule should be predictable and regular.

» *Stabilize in stages.* Open-source developers typically have access to at least three program builds at any on time: the most recent "development" build (which may not work properly), the most recent stable build (which is used for quality assurance), and the most recent "release-quality" build – the one that customers use.

» *Admit to yourself that you're running parallel development projects.* These three builds progress at different speeds, and as the program grows in complexity or as new ideas are proposed, careful judgment is required as to when a development build should be taken to another level.

» *Make major architectural leaps.* Incremental development is fine until major architectural changes are required. Periodically rebuilding the architecture, and researching new tools and standards enables you to ease the transition from old to new structures.

» *The key is talented, interested people* – "The pay-off to all the work we have done in setting up tools for distributed development will be the scalability that we get from a new, worldwide network of contributors," says Singleton. "The talent pool is very deep when you can draw from developers around the world, not just from a single city or a single company. A globally distributed team can include developers who are not only talented, but also interested in and knowledgeable about the task at hand."

» *Develop a trading economy.* During the development project engage customers directly in testing builds and suggesting their own desired enhancements, customizations and modifications, which can then be developed to benefit the wider community of users.

However, it must be remembered that these are early days in the development of these public/private strategies. Open-source developers rarely conform to a schedule, often relying on rough goals rather than hard delivery dates, making it hard for a commercial developer to plan a project. However, open-source expert Ken Coar (a member of the Apache Web Server group) contends that deadline-setting does make a difference even in the free and easy world of distributed open-source development. "Most open-source fixes will not be proposed until a release date (for the project) is announced," he says. The existence of a deadline triggers action in the open source community. (Steve Jobs had a telling motto for developers at Apple Computer, "Real Artists Ship." It's no good being a genius if you don't meet the production deadlines.)

OUTSOURCING AND OPEN SOURCING

The marriage of conventional software design procedures with open-source methods could produce a radical alternative to traditional outsourcing: perhaps *open sourcing* might best describe it. That open sourcing could be a valuable component in the e-innovation process there is no doubt, but the devil is in the detail. Needs vary, and there is currently no standard way of integrating the two modes – thus the importance of the experimental developments at IBM and Cambridge Interactive. How successful the open-sourcing model is remains to be seen, but distributed collaboration on creative projects will be an important element of e-innovation, and will demand a mix of video and web conferencing tools, shared resources and groupware tools that allow the multiparty interactive exploration of common models.

Back in the early 1960s, the ARPANET guru Joseph Licklider suggested that the solution to creative communication was the ability to collaboratively model problems and issues and simultaneously to share this common model with others. This is the crux of the kind of tools for "distributed innovation" that will mark out e-innovation from simple distributed sourcing. The creation of common tools, portals giving access to information and documentation, architecture schematics, code libraries and other resources is part of this, but the upcoming advent of broadband and the person-to-person communications channels it promises will see distributed collaborative innovation – e-innovation – really take off.

> "For modeling, we believe, is basic and central to communication. Any communication between people about the same thing is a common revelatory experience about informational models of that thing. Each model is a conceptual structure of abstractions formulated initially in the mind of one of the persons who would communicate, and if the concepts in the mind of one would-be communicator are very different from those in the mind of another, there is no common model and no communication."
>
> *Joseph Licklider (1960)*[2]

NOTES

1 Kogut, Bruce and Meitu, Anca (2000) *The Emergence of E-innovation: Insights from Open-Source Software Development* (working paper of the Reginald F. Jones Center, The Wharton School). University of Pennsylvania, PA.

2 Licklider, Joseph (1960) *Man–Computer Symbiosis* at http://www.memex.org/licklider.html

The State of the Art

» Networked innovation
» The groupware "ideal"
» A Master's in e-innovation
» The art of innovation
» Entrepreneurial innovation: Cybiko
» Bottom-up and open source
» The open net
» The vision of networked innovation
» The emergence of open source
» A giant bottom-up innovation machine.

Planning for e-innovation is top of the agenda in many institutions right now – and not just in the global media corporations at the leading edge of establishing new product ranges, new infrastructure, and new business models to optimize their business in the broadband, networked era. Small to medium-sized enterprises, start-ups – and even micro-businesses – are also engaged in the process of planning and developing strategies to ensure success in this rapidly evolving, technology-driven marketplace. While the biggest impact of digital media and networking developments will be felt most immediately by vendors of digital content – software, publishing, television broadcasters, video publishers, and music publishers, and by the advertising business that supports many of these enterprises – sooner rather than later other businesses and organizations will be forced to address these issues.

Strategic planning for the switch from atoms to bits, and for creating and developing successful products and services to compete in the bit marketplace, involves the integration of a number of previously disparate but overlapping disciplines, including:

» design and problem solving
» software design
» technology scoping and forecasting
» lifestyle trend analysis and forecasting
» market research
» new product development
» business planning.

The holistic nature of e-innovation practice suggests that this will be a process involving multidisciplinary teams. That the Web/Net itself provides the means by which to assemble such teams, and to facilitate their collaboration, means that e-innovators will need to explore a range of collaborative tools by which this process might most efficiently developed. The tools encompass a variety of proprietary and open-source "groupware", conferencing, and collaborative modeling applications.

NETWORKED INNOVATION

There are a number of groupware tools currently available, ranging from familiar, and often free, web-based tools such as e-mail, BBS, chat and ICQ messaging services, to sophisticated proprietary products such as Lotus Notes, Novell Groupwise and Microsoft NetMeeting. Over the last few years, there's been growing activity in this area as developers strive to create an easy-to-use, powerful application that integrates various combinations of conferencing, whiteboard, project management, content management, shared applications, collaborative modeling, and other desirable groupware features.

Microsoft's NetMeeting might be a good place to start exploring the potential of groupware – it's free for a start, and comes bundled with Windows 98 and 2000, as well as some webcam hardware packages. NetMeeting uses separate screen windows for video conferencing input, text chat, whiteboard and other facilities, but can only support one-to-one video conferencing, although at quite a high quality. By contrast, the CUSeeMe Networks $75 CUSeeMe Pro software presents a more integrated GUI (graphical user interface), combining video monitors from multiple video and audio participants together with text chat and participant listings, other functions such as whiteboard, shared application areas, and file transfer appear in separate windows. But there are many groupware products both available and in development, and one of the first tasks for e-innovation teams is to survey and appraise these different offerings.

The groupware "ideal"

The ideal is easier to define than to find. Broadband networking (DSL, cable and wireless networking systems) will improve the body language communication potential of such applications – providing much better quality video and audio conferencing for many simultaneous participants, as well as near-real-time collaborative white-boards and application sharing. The ideal is based on Joseph Licklider's vision – as expressed in his seminal papers on the computer as a communications device and what he called *man–computer symbiosis* – that applications that offer shared collaborative modeling using graphic, schematic and other modeling techniques to elaborate problems are the key to liberating the power of networking in distributed problem solving.

Of course, open-source and outsourcing or distributed software development techniques could be applied in this area, notably in the modularization of tasks and the parceling-out of these tasks to special interest groups. This strategy will, of course, require powerful, multi-source integration or "idea-compositing" tools (and human editorial expertise) as well as project management tools. In the longer term, we might see tools that allow both the harnessing of human expertise from remote sources and access to smart databases or expert systems embodying knowledge from many experts.

Ultimately we can imagine applications that facilitate the ability to participate in multiparty brainstorming sessions with access not only to Web-based search engines and agents, but to expert systems too, perhaps coupled with the kind of eye-contact video conferencing described by VR pioneer Jaron Lanier in a recent *Scientific American* feature, entitled "Virtually There" (online at www.sciam.com/2001/0401issue/0401lanier.html). This feature describes developments in tracking eye-ball positions of video conferencing participants to provide virtual eyeball-to-eyeball experiences. Broadband networking, with its round-the-clock connectivity ("always on" connections) offers opportunities for really spontaneous and casual dialogue, together with the means to deliver our body language signals (the gestures, facial expressions and so on that characterize real-world conversations) in high-definition video, promises to allow the kind of tele-presence experiences essential to meaningful conferencing and groupware. The aim is to generate in the tele-presence world the "serotonin effect" that amplifies our experience of real meetings with people in the real world, by means of high-definition communications giving us a heightened sense of contact and proximity. This sense of presence and proximity in groupware will further amplify the experience of communicating across different cultures and languages. Spoken languages often do not translate well, whereas facial expressions communicate the same message almost universally. Broadband networking will build body language and emotion into the groupware dialogue.

A Master's in e-innovation

Awareness of the potential of e-innovation processes is naturally emerging in the educational sector – in management schools as well as in media design schools. I recently appraised a proposed master's degree in "Future Communications" at the University of Ulster. Aimed at communications designers, and users of design in all communications sectors, the proposed course rationale indicates the e-innovation potential here:

"Opportunities in the communications field are changing – [the lesson is] change faster or disappear. Technology offers opportunity beyond its current use profile. There is currently a lack of integral thinking in many professional situations. There are more opportunities for innovation than are currently being exploited because of traditional models of production and delivery."[1]

And the educational aims and objectives clarify Ulster's approach to e-innovation:

"The MSc in Future Communications is for people who have understood that they work in a society undergoing exponential change, who refuse to be victims of change, and who want to use communications efficiently to help shape the future – for society, for the organizations where they work, and for themselves. The course enables this by providing a proactive context and environment which fosters synergy and innovative thinking in ways of creating, producing and applying communication material. This environment is structured to encourage a culture of enquiry which identifies the opportunities created by evolving cyber technologies, societies and practices and explores the potential resulting from change in relation to these elements. It provides a forum where communication practitioners can engage with contemporary issues and focus thinking on ways of broadening the context of the communication process in future practice."[1]

The proposed course is a mix of theory and practical work covering the spectrum of issues relevant to e-innovation, and including technology analysis and forecasting, innovation and design practice, and planning innovation, and culminates with a major project synthesizing research theory and practice in outlining an area of investigation that the student believes has the potential for innovation in the field of communications design. This investigation is delivered as dissertation or as a text-supported prototype or working model.

Is such a course important? The courseware designers are seasoned new media practitioners, well aware that the pressures of daily deadlines mitigate against the kind of innovation seeking, problem solving, and creativity that requires perspective and "play" time to emerge. They are aware that many businesses under-optimize their creative resources, missing much of the potential for innovation in the daily hustle. The Future Media course is designed to allow senior designers and creatives time to refocus and relocate themselves in this "opportunity space." (For more on opportunity space see Chapter 7, E-Innovation in Practice.)

THE ART OF INNOVATION

Just as a jazz musician extemporizes, invents, and innovates to the structured accompaniment of his fellow musicians, so the input of creative designers, engineers, and thinkers will be facilitated and amplified by a structured e-innovation process. The harnessing of holistic research, technology forecasting, creative vision, market research, the ability to synergize and represent ideas, and to plan, design, and develop them through to profitable products or services – these are the objectives of e-innovation. We can create structures and methodologies that lubricate the creative process and that enhance, amplify, augment, and help manage and record the process. We can reduce the odds against failure. We can create the conditions where innovation is most likely to flourish. Indeed this is what designers, entrepreneurs, scientists, engineers, and inventors have done throughout our history.

E-innovators can learn lessons from the investigative analyses and experimental processes of science, from the problem-solving and solution-exploration methodology of design, from the bisociation of disparate ideas and inverted logic in comedy, from the lateral, non-linear exploration and interpretation of nature and life in art, from all the various creative stratagems and practical and experimental wizardry of magic, and indeed from all aspects of our culture where the new emerges from an effort to understand, explain, and demonstrate better ways of doing, of seeing and of understanding. The analysis of these methodologies and their composite development as processes to enhance innovation in the real-time, networked world is central to the art of innovation. But innovation doesn't just stop with the idea for the killer application, or with its expression in a prototype or model. Creativity must permeate and inform every stage of the innovation process, from corporate strategic planning down to modularized programming and on to productivization, promotion, marketing, distribution, and production management.

The importance of networking is paramount in this process. It is no accident that, historically, great art emerged from periods of history when great artists grouped together in particular locations – Florence in the fifteenth century, Paris in the late nineteenth, Switzerland during the First World War, New York during the Second. Great work emerges from the proximity and interlocution (networking) of peers. Replicating this creative clustering on the Web/Net, intranet or virtual private network is the promise of high-bandwidth groupware.

Entrepreneurial innovation: the example of Cybiko – do it fast and do it better

The history of innovation is informative. And it's not only about leading-edge engineers inventing new technologies. It's also a kind of "outsider", "edge" or bottom-up process in which new configurations of technologies and human needs are brought into confluence – and profit – by perceptive entrepreneurs. David Yang is one such entrepreneur and Cybiko one such product. Identifying the new product or service opportunities in the interstices of various strands of technological development, seeing the gap in the market for them, putting available technologies together in affordable packages to address this market, and creating infectious enthusiasm for the product is the dream ticket of innovation, and Yang did just this with Cybiko.

Yang founded Cybiko Inc in Moscow in 1999. With a background in AI software development, Yang was already running a successful software company. The insight for Cybiko? *Put the Game Boy together with the mobile.* Yang realized the enormous potential of a wireless personal games machine that could also allow users to communicate with other gamers, as well as to download free games from the Web, or swap games with other machines. So he invented just such a device. ("Invention" here is the art of bringing together several technologies into a new combination.)

Cybiko is a small, cheap ($185), plastic hand-held computer. It doesn't use expensive cellular networking, instead using short-range radio, offering instant voice contact with other Cybiko owners within range (100–200 meters outdoor range in US, and up to 1 kilometer range in Europe). This is fun, but there's more. Cybiko messages can hop from one Cybiko machine to another, creating a peer-to-peer network where two people can communicate over large (well, metropolitan) distances through the network of Cybikos. Because it uses low-power, short-range radio, text messaging is free. And with a memory plug-in and PC connection, Cybiko can download e-mail too, synchronizing with Outlook 2000 on the PC. Cybiko Inc uploads new games to its Website every day, adding to the pool of 200 already created. Games are free too. Users download them to a PC and copy them to the Cybiko – or get copies wirelessly from other Cybiko "intertainment" machines.

In February 2001, the UK's *Guardian* newspaper reported that this Russian-designed machine, manufactured in Taiwan, with software and games written in Moscow, and the promise of more games supplied by an international network of games developers, was "spreading across the US like influenza." By February, 500,000 Cybikos had sold in the US, and the company was planning an "adult" version, providing organizer facilities – directly challenging Palm, the market leader.

Yang's "network effect" thinking extends to embrace wide industry partnerships – with backing from Sun Technology and AOL Investments and with AOL providing the instant messaging technology. Cybiko Inc will also make Cybiko plug-ins for Palms and other handhelds – thereby expanding still further the value of the Cybiko network. Metcalfe's Law (that "each new node squares the value of the network") suggests that the more Cybiko owners there are, the greater will be the functionality – and fun and funkiness – that the Cybiko network offers; and of course Cybiko hopes that this will be a self-generating or "viral marketing" effect – that this effect will reach critical mass, where the Cybiko is seen to be a must-have accessory by kids on the street.

Just as Palm and Handspring brought new thinking to the hand-held arena and succeeded by applying brilliant design and product development to a product designed to meet real people's real needs, so the Cybiko tapped the messaging/gaming zeitgeist for the kids.

As a counter example of top-down planning for change, consider Sony Corporations grand plan for the broadband networked era. (See Chapter 7, E-Innovation in Practice.)

BOTTOM-UP AND OPEN SOURCE

It's worth examining this bottom-up approach to e-innovation much further here, not only because this was how the whole Internet thing was developed in the first place, but because many would argue that these bottom-up (or "edge-inwards") innovations are the future of our highly networked, highly processor-mediated economy, and our main protection against the monopolistic tendencies of the mega-corporation proprietary software developers. The underpinning ethos of bottom-up innovation is that of the Net itself – the openness and cooperation that characterizes the blossoming open-source movement, the idea that superior software results not from proprietary "private" code development, but in the free publication and open development of public license software.

The open Net

The development of the Internet was one of America's great gifts to humanity, easily outranking those other great US gifts of jazz, rock 'n' roll, and jeans, as contributions to our world culture. In the late 1950s and 60s, the US Government pumped funding into the emerging technologies of computing, networking, and software, creating a special government agency to ensure that these funds were directed to the researchers most able to contribute to US success in these fields. The Advanced Research Projects Agency or ARPA was created in the wake of the sputnik scare of 1959, when in the most public and global demonstration possible to imagine, the USSR showed that – in space technology at least – it was ahead of the US.

The threat of nuclear airborne attack in the 1950s had led to the development of the SAGE computerized radar early-warning system, and had spurred the development of advanced, transistorized computers capable of real-time operations. Other by-products of the nuclear threat were the development of game theory, cybernetics, systems theory and scenario-planning in US universities, research centers and at the new "think tanks" such as the Rand Corporation and the Hudson Institute. It was in a series of papers written for the Rand Corporation during the early 1960s that Paul Baran first proposed a new national network of computers that would provide a bombproof communications system, capable of sustaining military and Government communications in the aftermath of a nuclear attack. These papers, especially perhaps his 1962 report "On Distributed Communications Networks", marked the beginning of a decade of development work on what was to become the Internet.

In this US Air Force-funded report, Baran first outlined the principle of the "redundancy of connectivity", and explored various models of communications systems, evaluating their vulnerability. His report proposed a network that had no vulnerable central hub, and in which all surviving nodes would be able to re-establish contact with each other. One of his recommendations was for a new national public utility to carry computer data – allowing remote computers to "talk" to each other in much the same way that the telephone network allowed people to talk to each other, but with no vulnerable centralized exchanges. Baran asked:

> "Is it time now to start thinking about a new and possibly non-existent public utility, a common user digital data communication plant designed specifically for the transmission of digital data among a large set of subscribers?"
>
> *David Ellis (1998)[2]*

Baran argued that such a network should not be based on public telephone networks, and that it would require a more innovative solution. In a number of papers (about 11 in all), Baran proposed a "store and forward" packetized solution for data communications that would come to known as packet switching. (It was so called by UK networking pioneer Donald Davies, a couple of years later.)

Packet switching is a delightfully simple idea. Before transmission through a computer network, the data (words, sound, programs, pictures, etc. in digital form) are segmented into "packets" of equal length. Each packet is numbered, and contains a "header" of information describing where it is going (the address of the recipient), where it is from, the total number of packets in the transmission, and the number of the particular packet. There was also an error-correction mechanism – a number representing the total number of bits in the packet. On transmission, each packet is passed from one computer to another through the system until it reaches the recipient. Each computer in the network reads the header, checks that the packet is still intact, and passes it on to the next link in the direction of the recipient. The final recipient computer checks that it has received the total number of packets in the transmission, then compiles them in the correct order. If one or more packets is missing, a message is sent back to the originating computer asking for a re-send.

Sending out packets in this way meant that only one packet need arrive for the receiver to know how to request the others. It also meant that packets could be routed around non-functioning nodes – effectively a self-healing system. Of course, such a network required the development of a common protocol, and "routers" that could direct packets in the most efficient way, temporarily "storing" packets before "forwarding" them to the next node.

The efforts to design and build such technologies took nearly a decade, and consumed considerable ARPA funds. The result was the launch of ARPANET in 1969. (It became the Internet during the early 1970s, as ARPANET grew and began to interconnect other networks linking campuses throughout the US and Europe). As a result of this public-funded R&D during the 1960s, most of what we take for granted in modern computing was imagined, invented, and developed, or at least prototyped (for example, hypertext, e-mail, word processing, groupware, screen windows, the mouse, computer graphics and computer simulation – were all developed or conceived in the 1960s). And all these innovations were in the public domain – shared between developers in the open, reciprocal manner that had characterized developments in science since time immemorial.

The vision of networked innovation

A linchpin in these developments was Joseph Licklider, whose important 1960 paper on "Man–Computer Symbiosis" led to his appointment as a director of ARPA, and directly inspired many of the computing pioneers. Licklider's vision was extraordinary. He was the first to glimpse the potential of networking and of easy-to-use computer interfaces in fostering innovation and creative collaboration. He wrote:

> "The hope, is that in not too many years, human brains and computing machines will be coupled ever more tightly, and that the resulting partnership will think as no human brain has ever thought and process data in a way not approached by the information-handling machines we know today."

> *Joseph Licklider (1960)[3]*

In a later paper Licklider and his co-author wrote:

> "In a few years men will be able to communicate more effectively through a machine than face to face...When minds interact, new ideas emerge."

> *Joseph Licklider and Robert Taylor (1969)[4]*

In his role as a project director at ARPA, Licklider was able to analyze and direct many of the seminal developments that characterize modern computing and networking, and that encouraged open collaboration on software and hardware innovation.

The emergence of open source

As Nathan Newman points out in his NetAction white paper:

> "One key (ARPA) project was a $3 million per year grant to Project MAC at MIT to encourage the spread of time-sharing computing on the then-breakthrough minicomputer technology. ARPA would fund six of the first twelve time-sharing computer systems in the country, which in turn would help spark the whole minicomputer industry in the 1960s – crucial in the industry and the Boston-area regional economy then but as crucial to the development of the Internet over the next decades. Out of Project MAC would largely develop the early ethos of software and hardware innovation – "hacking" in its early non-pejorative sense before it became confused with electronic vandalism – that launched the computer

revolution. It was MIT hackers at Project MAC who largely designed both hardware and software for DEC's breakthrough PDP-6 time-sharing minicomputer. They would spend endless hours creating and sharing new software to extend its capabilities beyond the expectations of its creators."

Nathan Newman (1999)[5]

The culture of cooperation and sharing amongst computer scientists and "hackers" that grew out of MIT and ARPA also became the norm at Stanford on the West Coast (where the mouse was invented in 1968 by Douglas Engelbart, on another ARPA project), and so on throughout the emerging Silicon Valley hardware and software businesses that this great center of excellence spun-off from the 1950s onwards. And later, by means of the new networks, this culture spread to every software development locus on the planet. Suddenly the "economies of agglomeration" became location-free. (Economies of agglomeration are the economic benefits that small businesses enjoy from the concentration of many of them in a particular city or other location – they include the benefits of social networking: shoptalk from chance meetings, news networking and filtering, and gossip, as well as benefits that accrue from the local growth of mutually shared service industries.)

The network became the agglomeration. E-mail, newsgroups and bulletin boards carried the shoptalk. In private (commercial) and publicly-funded institutions and businesses alike, the flow-through of skilled staff (the engineers and software designers who constitute the pool of resources to businesses, organizations, and other employers), also bound both public and private sector into the underpinning ethos of openness and "coopetition." Perpetuating the same code of ethics, Tim Berners Lee convinced CERN to freely publish his World Wide Web software in 1991.

A giant bottom-up innovation machine

All the conditions for clusters of creativity are nurtured by the Net. It is a giant, bottom-up, innovation machine as well as a medium by which and through which distributed, centralized software developments may be propagated and managed.

The 1980s saw the emergence of the large-scale use of proprietary software as computer use shifted to personal computers. The open-architecture PC and MSDOS (the first PC standard operating system) were challenged by the proprietary code and hardware of Apple Computer and their Macintosh computer and operating system. During the 1980s and 90s, as Microsoft developed Windows, their proprietary commercial software came to dominate the marketplace. Then along came the (publicly funded) Web, and the first (publicly funded) browsers – notably Mosaic, developed at the University of Illinois – and open standards began to re-emerge to challenge the dominant proprietary software hegemonies. However, in the 90s the whole culture of Federal funding, and the Federal guarding of open standards, was in decline (as a result of the end of the Cold War, as well as the effects of Reaganism) – and there was no centralized body supporting open standards.

So it wasn't surprising that first Netscape and then Microsoft tried to seize control of publicly funded open standards (for example, building browsers that provided for non-standard HTML code). Microsoft was arraigned on anti-trust charges, and Netscape decided in 1998 to publish its browser source-code – to make it open source.

In a brief history of the open source initiative,[6] the authors describe how this Netscape announcement provided the opportunity for them to present the case for open-source development:

"The 'open source' label itself came out of a strategy session held on February 3rd 1998 in Palo Alto, California. The people present included Todd Anderson, Chris Peterson (of the Foresight Institute)[7], John 'maddog' Hall and Larry Augustin (both of Linux International)[8], Sam Ockman (of the Silicon Valley Linux User's Group), and Eric Raymond. We were reacting to Netscape's announcement[9] that it planned to give away the source of its browser. One of us (Raymond)[10] had been invited out by Netscape to help them plan the release and follow-on actions. We realized that the Netscape announcement had created a precious window of time within which we might finally be able to get the corporate world to listen to what we have to teach about the superiority of an open development process. We realized it was time to dump the confrontational attitude that has been associated with 'free software' in the past and sell the idea strictly on the same pragmatic, business-case grounds that motivated Netscape."

The open-source initiative is in full swing, buoyed by the success of three open-source software projects:

» Linux – Linus Torvalds' open version of the underpinning Internet software, Unix (Linux enjoys a 40% share of the Unix operating system marketplace, with approximately 17 million users worldwide);
» Apache – the open-source server software (Apache is used by around 60% of servers); and
» Java – invented by Sun Microsystems, but now enjoying open-source status as a platform-independent programming language supported by and contributed to by developers all around the world.

The more gung ho evangelizers for open source, such as Ganesh Prasad, cheerfully forecast the death of proprietary software as open-source software development continues to prove that it is more stable, better documented, more frequently updated, and, above all, beats proprietary software hands down on price. In his article "The coming Java-Linux duopoly" Prasad forecasts:

"Open Source products cannot be defeated in the marketplace. They will become market leaders in every major software category in 3–5 years. Most successful devices will run Open Source operating systems and basic Open Source applications like browsers and mail clients."

Ganesh Prasad (2000)[11]

Open-source thinking permeates the software development community worldwide. It is a philosophy growing directly from the US Government funding of the Internet, and from the much older tradition of academic and scientific information-sharing, and it won't go away. Open source, enabled by the Web/Net, and by hardware-independent operating systems and languages like Linux and Java, will provide the wellspring from which e-innovators will draw inspiration and tap into a global pool of software engineering talent.

As has been mentioned in other sections, e-innovation is likely to take two main directions, using open-source development methods, and using the Web/Net to outsource modularized software development. But there is a third way, too – the centralized, strategically directed, internal innovation of the world's leading hardware and software companies.

NOTES

1 University of Ulster (2001) *Master of Science in Future Communications* Evaluation Proposal. Faculty of Arts, University of Ulster, Belfast.

2 Ellis, David (1998) *A History of Usenet* at http://ucsub.colorado.edu/~ellisda/usenet/usenet.html

3 Licklider, Joseph (1960) *Man–Computer Symbiosis* at http://www.memex.org/licklider.html

4 Licklider, Joseph and Taylor, Robert (1969) *The Computer as Communications Device* at http://www.memex.org/licklider.html

5 Newman, Nathan (1999) *The Origins and Future of Open Source Software* at http://www.netaction.org/opensrc/future/oss-whole.html#create

6 http://www.opensource.org/docs/history.html

7 http://www.foresight.org/

8 http://www.li.org/

9 http://www.netscape.com/newsref/pr/newsrelease558.html

10 http://tuxedo.org/~esr/

11 Prasad, Ganesh (2000) *The coming Java-Linux duopoly*. At www.linuxdevices.com/articles/AT7102892618.html

E-Innovation in Practice

E-innovation success stories:

» Entrepreneurial and strategic innovation
» The MP3 opportunity space
» MP3.com
» The ultimate juke-box
» Diamond's Rio
» The "suck-it and see" path to innovation
» Strategic innovation: Sony broadband strategy
» Towards the ubiquitous value network
» Strengthening Internet/communication services
» Tooling-up for the "era of 1 million publishers"
» Inventing the future at Sony computer science labs.

INTRODUCTION

I want to illustrate the diversity of approaches to e-innovation. Elsewhere (Key Concepts and Resources, Chapter 9) I describe the two main approaches used here, those of entrepreneurial innovation and strategic innovation – the one reflecting tactical immediacy and responsiveness to opportunity and "bottom-up" or "edge" opportunity spotting, the other a way of encouraging innovation thinking and opportunity spotting at all levels of the corporation, and of developing structures and methodologies that best underpin and support innovation.

Both of these approaches rely on information (market research, technology scoping, trend analysis, etc.) and on the skills of entrepreneurs, executives, managers, developers and designers in identifying opportunities in the emerging matrix of possibilities – and acting upon them rapidly. I have called the information-analysis phase of innovation (Chapter 9) "mapping the opportunity space", and suggest visual and collaborative approaches to this process. Now I want to look at how three different entrepreneurs approached the opportunity space created by a new audio media standard: MP3 in the late 1990s.

THE MP3 OPPORTUNITY SPACE

In 1997, after several years of development and refining, the Motion Pictures Experts Group (a group of individuals representing over 200 companies worldwide) published the specification for an advanced audio-compression encoding format. The MPEG Level 3 Advanced Audio Coding provided digital audio users with high quality encoding and a small file size. It came to be known as MP3, and proved to be the ideal Web/Net medium for high quality digital audio (music) files, providing a quality that made previous popular digital audio file formats sound really tinny, and providing this quality in small file sizes. The MPEG Level 3 Advanced Audio Coding (MP3) file format was declared an international standard by MPEG at the end of April 1997. Music fans quickly recognized that MP3 was vastly superior both in quality, and in compression, to previous file formats such as WAV and AVI, and a number of tools for processing digital audio files into MP3 became available on the Web (often as free downloads) through 1997–98, many of which were suitable for use by non-technical users. MP3 began to be used widely as a means of compressing and storing music tracks digitally.

People began swapping their favorite music tracks across the Web, and as MP3 increased in popularity, the opportunity space expanded rapidly. Opportunities included (and still include): MP3 Websites, file-conversion tools, MP3 file Web search engines, software jukeboxes and players for PCs and handheld access devices, Net-based MP3 file-storage services, copyright tagging and tracking software, MP3 multimedia enhancements (pictures, text, graphics, etc.), artists' direct publishing, record industry A&R (artistes and repertoire – record business talent spotting) services, specific record genre collections and subscription services, and using MP3 files as samplers for direct marketing of CDs. But in the longer term, MP3 is much more important. It was the first people-to-people "content" medium. MP3 networks, whether centralized through a particular Web service or "peer to peer", clearly indicate a distribution model that will impact upon all other media. E-books will be distributed, promoted, and sold this way and, when broadband is viable, movies and television will follow. So the developers of MP3 network distribution intuited that their technologies might play a seminal role in the future of all media, not just music.

In this section I want to look at how three entrepreneurs – an 18-year-old first timer, a 30-year-old with two moderately successful companies under his belt and a 60-something at the head of a £600mn multimedia and video card company – addressed this opportunity.

MP3.com

A number of entrepreneurs spotted the MP3 opportunities – and several entrepreneurs built successful businesses from MP3. Thirty-year-old Michael Robertson was one. A young entrepreneur with two software companies already under his belt, Robertson spotted the first opportunity and registered and founded MP3.com, a Website for music fans using MP3. Robertson built his business by featuring downloads of MP3 tracks donated freely by unsigned artists. This gave musicians and composers direct access to a wide and adventurous audience, and a chance to market CDs to them, and gave consumers access to tens of thousands of music tracks. By March 2000, around 170 artists were signing up per day at MP3.com, and tens of millions of MP3 tracks had been downloaded. Since then, MP3.com has continued to innovate by offering the My.MP3.com service, which lets people store their music online at the MP3.com Website.

The ultimate juke-box

The idea here is truly visionary – MyMP3.com is Robertson's vision of the "ultimate juke-box" – the day when music lovers all over the world will store their personal record collections on the Web (hopefully on MP3.com), so they (a) never lose records, (b) can access them from any Web/Net access device anywhere in the world (from mobile PDAs, to in-car Web-enabled stereos, to PCs, portable players, hotel radio alarms, etc.), and (c) build a really personal "always-on" collection that provides the music or song you want, when you want it.

MP3.com was an instant success and still averages about 100,000 hits a day. It features a ratings chart for MP3 music. The ratings are based on the number of downloads a song attracts. The site also provides tutorials and guides to MP3, how it can be used to encode audio tracks copied from CDs, as well as editorials and news, and links to other sites for software players and MP3 downloads. There are currently over 150,000 artists from more than 180 countries that make their music available to music fans through MP3.com. And what's more, more than 25% of *Billboard Magazine*'s current Top 40 albums are being promoted on the site. Before 2001, the MP3.com business model was sponsored and carried "advertising-supported content", though they were already planning for subscription services, launching the MP3.com classical music channel in May 2000. At that time Robertson enthused, "It's a great program for any classical music fan. They can go to MP3.com, pay $9.99 a month, and get complete access to an entire classical music library of about 400 albums that they can download, playback, and organize any way they want. So, we're kind of mirroring what TV and cable did for the movie world, but for music."

As the RIAA (Recording Industry Association of America) and the five major labels clamp down on the infringement of their copyrights, so we will inevitably see the MP3 file-distribution model move from purely ad-supported to subscription/encryption models. Later, when e-cash and other easy to use micropayment systems become available, there will be a (digital) cash market here too. Like other MP3 developers and distributors, MP3.com faced litigation from the music industry, including copyright infringement proceedings initiated by Vivendi Universal. But Robertson could see the future. He knew that MP3.com's technology was going to be of seminal importance to the industry – and the industry knew it too.

And MP3.com has developed considerable proprietary technology for the delivery of online music, including the development of a "music inter-operating system" (IOS), designed to provide a common platform for the music business, by connecting retailers, labels, music players, and hardware and software tools. MP3.com claims that Music IOS is fully compatible with a variety of devices and networks, and that the company also possesses proprietary, patented technology for music distribution as well as comprehensive solutions in data management and tracking. MP3.com's proven distribution technology can power not only music, but also video and text content.

So after suing MP3.com for copyright infringement, in May 2001 Vivendi Universal (the second largest media company after AOL Time Warner) acquired MP3.com for $372mn, with the intent of creating a legal music-distribution network to rival the Bertelsmann/Napster service. Universal Vivendi is in a joint venture with Sony to create a new Net-based music distribution/subscription service called Duet, and it looks like MP3.com technology will drive Duet.

DIAMOND'S RIO

Another part of the MP3 opportunity space was identified by Chong Moon Lee, the 64-year-old founder and chairman of Diamond Multimedia, a $600mn manufacturer of video cards and other multimedia hardware. Lee saw the potential for a small, portable, solid-state MP3 player that would allow users to copy MP3 files from their PCs and use just like a Walkman. The confluence of technologies for such a device was fortuitous. Flash memory chips (that store data in solid-state memory) were becoming much more widely available at affordable prices, especially the 32 Mb chips that could store 30 minutes of MP3 music. Because there are no moving parts (no tape or disk drives), solid-state players are much lighter on battery power, and are "judder free" for hectic social use – they don't skip when you're dancing or jogging. Interestingly, just before Diamond made their Rio announcement, IBM had launched Microdrive – a miniscule hard drive – small enough to fit into a portable player and capable of storing 340 Mb of data, but these were still relatively expensive, relatively power hungry, and susceptible to skipping. (However, Diamond planned to use Microdrive in future Rio players.) Diamond also had developed considerable expertise in digital-signal processing technology, and already had the manufacturing clout to tool up for and produce a player. Diamond announced that they would be launching a sub-$200 solid-state MP3 player in October 1998. And what's more, to the recording industry's chagrin, they would ship free software that would enable users to convert CD tracks to MP3 files.

The RIAA slapped an injunction on Diamond "to preliminarily enjoin Diamond Multimedia from distributing their Rio player based on allegations that the Rio violated the Audio Home Recording Act of 1992." Diamond successfully fought this injunction, arguing that the Rio player was not an archiving device and that the Flash media it used were (at $50 a pop) unlikely to encourage illegal music trading.

Diamond started a huge bush fire – there were over 155 million portable MP3 units sold to consumers in the year 2000. And, as the first popular MP3 portable player, the Rio showed the future of personal media access: it introduced the idea that media (not just music) could be available anywhere you wanted it. To support the Rio, Diamond had developed RioPort – the name for both the companion software used to manage MP3 files on the Rio, and for the Website www.rioport.com, which offered a music track download service available to anyone, but with more integrated MP3 downloads and software-updating especially for Rio owners. This software is a suite containing music library tools, a RIPer/encoder (application that creates MP3 from CDs), a synchronization utility, and a built-in Web browser that connects directly with rioport.com and other popular MP3 sites. MP3 files can be downloaded, managed and arranged in the PC library software, and then synched with a connected Rio.

Diamond Multimedia was acquired by S3 Corporation in September 1999, and rioport.com was spun off as a separate company a month later. Rioport.com's major investor is S3, and the company's main focus will be the further development of back end digital media distribution systems and related software. MP3.com had already pointed up the opportunities here.

THE SUCK-IT-AND-SEE PATH TO INNOVATION?

Perhaps the classic example of the possibilities of bottom-up, and the antithesis of planned, innovation is the "suck it and see" approach of 20-year-old Shawn Fanning in his development of Napster, the music file-sharing program. In June 1999, Fanning (a college drop-out, like Bill Gates) uploaded his beta version Napster program to the Website he shared with a friend. Fanning had some programming experience picked up at his uncle John Fanning's online gaming company, and at NorthEastern University in Boston. Like many of his online contemporaries, he was a great fan of MP3 – the high-quality, high-compression music file format that enabled CD-quality music tracks to be efficiently downloaded through the Web. Napster was conceived by Fanning as a better way of finding and downloading MP3 files than using conventional search engines and FTP (file-transfer protocol). John Fanning incorporated Napster in May 1999 with himself and Shawn as 70/30 shareholders.

In June, Shawn Fanning invited about 30 chat-room friends to try the program, on the condition that they kept it to themselves. But as soon as they had tried it, they couldn't resist spreading the word. In less than a week between 3–4000 others had downloaded Napster from Fanning's Website. Armed with this evidence of Napster's power, John Fanning began working on the first round of funding for the company, approaching friends and raising about 6 month's worth of funding selling the first "A" round of Napster equity for 10 cents a share. By September, friends had invested some $350,000 more.

In the spring of that year, John Fanning had begun to consult the leading intellectual property attorney Andrew P. Bridges, who had successfully defended Diamond Multimedia Systems in the Rio case when they had been sued for encouraging copyright transgressions by the RIAA. During this time, Fanning decided that, if it came to the crunch, he could successfully defend Napster against legal action.

By the fall of 1999, Napster was enjoying the fruits of the instant distribution network process known as viral marketing. Napster soft-ware was selling itself in the self-igniting, wildfire success that marks out the impact of a true "killer app." A reputed 25 million people worldwide were busy filling up their local hard disk space and burning CD-ROMs with MP3 tracks, courtesy of Napster. In October 1999,

Napster raised $2mn in a series "B" round of angel funding from wealthy investors including Ron Conway of Angel Investors, and Joe Krauss (co-founder of Excite@Home), and the company made the move west to Silicon Valley, setting up shop in San Mateo, California.

The RIAA sued Napster on December 7, 1999, and while this complicated the process of attracting venture capital, it didn't stop Napster eventually raising $15mn from Hummer Winblad and, in May, it brought in Hummer partner Hank Barry as interim CEO. John Hummer also joined the Napster board. During summer 2000, Barry started molding the company into a business, hiring top music industry executive Milton Olin (ex senior vice-president at A&M Records) as chief operating officer, and engaging David Boies to join the legal defense team.

During this time Barry had renewed negotiations with the recording industry, pointing out how Napster technology could be used as a new distribution channel by the industry itself. But despite obvious (indeed overwhelming) consumer demand, a working and attractive technology, and capitalists and entrepreneurs ready to go, Barry couldn't resolve the industry's licensing concerns. The industry had two handicaps: a resistance to change, and the legacy licensing and IP issues with its artists. So they went to court and Napster lost. In June 2000, after only 15 minutes consideration, Judge Marilyn Hall Patel ruled that Napster had to remove all copyright-infringing materials from its service within the week.

Six months later, in October, Bertelsmann shocked the industry by agreeing to work with Napster in the creation of a subscription-based, street-legal service The deal was finessed by a Bertelsmann investment in Napster of more than $50mn, giving the German record group a majority share. The two companies agreed that Napster would continue to run some form of free service as well as the subscription service, which it predicted would be launched in June or July 2001. Napster meanwhile had introduced song-identification technology to filter copyright-protected songs from its service. By June 2001, Bertelsmann had managed to bring some other major labels on board, signing agreements that will allow Napster to sell music offered by MusicNet, a company created by the streaming media developer RealNetworks and three major labels: AOL-Time Warner's Warner Music Group, EMI Recorded Music and Bertelsmann Music Group.

In May 2001, the digital music distribution battle hotted-up with Vivendi Universal acquiring MP3.com with the intent of creating a legal music-distribution network to rival the Bertelsmann/Napster service. And Sony announced its intention of establishing an SDMI-based (encrypted) music networking service – all this while Napster is still bogged-down in litigation.

Why use Napster as an example of e-innovation? Doesn't "e-innovation" mean the process of productivizing (and profiting from) new technology? Of course it does. Napster is the classic counter-example, and catalogues what happens when e-innovation processes are effectively ignored. Napster had a revolutionary solution to music distribution online. They had a really popular product and launched it without wide (any?) music industry support, gambling on a *fait accompli*. They had an inexperienced CEO (before Hank Barry took over), who did not successfully present the Napster case to the music industry – a broad base of strategic partners is essential to successful e-innovation.

But the lessons of Napster are writ large, and other companies with innovative peer-to-peer networking plans are not slow to learn from them. For example, the developer WebMethods is developing an XML-based Web conferencing application – bringing easy to use and low-cost multiparty conferencing facilities to the Web/Net is the focus of considerable effort. It is another interesting "solution space" to explore.

STRATEGIC INNOVATION: SONY'S BROADBAND STRATEGY

In March 2001, Sony Corporation announced its intention to transform itself into a "personal broadband network solutions company" in preparation for the broadband network society that Sony sees emerging around 2005. Their published strategy for positioning the company in the broadband era is a revealing glimpse of how a major multinational is tooling up, not just for the imminent era of broadband networking, but for the era of continuous change.

The "personal" bit refers both to Sony's focus on the individual consumer and to the increasing capability of new media to be personalized (customized) by their users. "Broadband" refers to the next generation of Internet, mobile telecommunications, wired telecoms networks, and digital television (DTV) media channels that promise "anywhere, anytime, anything" 24-hours a day TV-quality connectivity. Broadband is defined roughly as a channel able to carry good quality, good size, TV images. Broadband media channels include GPRS and 3G mobile (cellular) networks, satellite DTV and datacasting, cable+fiber networks, and DSL telecoms networks, and Sony sees these new media channels and networks becoming a viable marketplace for their products by mid-decade. Their broadband strategy document pulls together the various strands of research and product development that have been a hallmark of Sony's digital thinking over the last few years, and indicates the infrastructural changes that Sony will implement to respond to the challenges of a rapidly evolving marketplace – a marketplace that Sony is betting will be characterized by ubiquitous broadband access and round-the-clock networking. But Sony's strategic thinking also includes how the company must adapt to the network economy. As Sony chairman and CEO Nobuyuki Idei said in December 1999:

> "E-business in the network era is rapidly changing. Electronic music distribution, for example, is becoming popular in the music business. Though technology continues to progress, as is the environment we operate in, I would like to stress that Sony's corporate philosophy, our desire to make 'products that are fun to use', remains unchanged. However, how Sony must adapt to the e-economy era, how we must be reborn as 'e-Sony' remains a critical, yet long-term theme that we must pursue along with current issues on how to restructure the electronics segment."
>
> *Nobuyuki Idei (1999)[1]*

Sony has already positioned itself for moves in the broadband direction with the development of integrated audio-video and computer products (such as VAIO), AV/IT convergence products (such as I-Link), the "4 network gateway" strategy (PlayStation 2, mobiles, VAIO and a set-top box), and the strengthening of their semiconductor/device developments and the creation of a network-compatible content business model. "Building on these achievements," said Idei, "Sony will continue to focus on and consolidate its unique resources in brand recognition, electronics, hardware expertise, entertainment business know-how and venture business development both within and outside the company. In enhancing group corporate value, we will pursue "soft alliances" with outside companies that will compliment our existing internal resources, and accelerate the pace of change."

Sony has five main strands to its global business, covering electronics, entertainment, games, Internet/communication services, and financial services, and its broadband strategy includes plans for changes in all these sectors, coordinated at the top by a reorganized headquarters centered on a "global hub" that focuses on overall management strategy, and that will provide a unified global vision and overall strategic management. The global hub will be led by the senior management team, comprising Noboyuki Idei (chairman and CEO), Kunitake Ando (president and COO) and Teruhisa Tokunaka (executive deputy president and CFO), whose tasks focus on the strategic unification of Sony's resources across all five main groups in the company, and on managing strategic proposals and far-reaching "think-tank" initiatives. To assist them in this task, a new Strategy Institute will be created, headed up by Akiyoshi Kawashima (corporate senior executive vice-president).

Sony are also planning a new management platform to offer consistent services in critical corporate staff functions such as accounting, legal, intellectual copyright, human resources, information systems, public relations, external affairs, and design. The intention here is to utilize networking and IT services and new work processes to deliver "speedy management" on a global scale.

Sony plans to develop their core electronics business by strengthening and enhancing product development and expanding the network connectivity of its electronics devices. All Sony's electronics-related business will be unified under a new electronics HQ. Kunitake Ando will steer this division. The principal initiatives announced in March 2001 included:

» *The integration of electronics, games, and Internet/communication services.* Sony are anticipating that game and Net/communication services will be deeply integrated with the consumer electronics hardware business in the broadband era, and it makes sense to integrate them in a single division in this way.

» *Reorganizing network companies (NCs) for the broadband era.* The five present NCs, organized along product lines, will be restructured into seven "solution-oriented" NCs. Resources will thus be directed into growth areas and authority further devolved to companies within the NCs in accordance with Sony's "integrated, decentralized" management system.

» *Introducing the horizontal platform concept.* Sony's network companies will be horizontally supported by three newly established technology centers, the engineering, manufacturing, and customer services platform and a sales platform (which includes both regional sales companies, and region-by-region-based Net direct-marketing). Sony hope that this will result in enhanced competitiveness and faster more efficient business practice.

The electronics business NC will follow Sony's extant "4 network gateway" strategy, based on Sony's forecast that the key broadband access devices (gateways) will include digital TVs and set-top boxes, mobile phones and PDAs, advanced VAIO computers, and PlayStation 2. (The games division currently contributes about 40% of Sony profits, and the PS2 has been designed specifically for broadband networking, including Ethernet to cable access, and I-link, as well as carrying an integrated DVD player.)

Towards the ubiquitous value network

The next goal is to develop a range of hardware that will best exploit the benefits of ubiquitous, "always on" broadband networking and that offers on-demand media and interactive communications. Sony's aim is to develop an array of electronics devices that can be seamlessly connected to each other and to the network. And further to this, Sony plans to integrate hardware with their content and services developments, to create a "ubiquitous value network" offering entertainment to their customers.

Developing hardware for the ubiquitous value network rests on two main developments:

» *Creating user-friendly hardware that integrates audiovisual and information technology, and the further development of mobile and home-network products that add communications technology to the existing AV/IT convergent product lines*. This would enable customers to access broadband content and services through a wide range of integrated access devices, players, monitors, etc. Sony are introducing IP (Internet Protocol) version 6.0 into all their hardware products. (IP 6.0 expands on the previous IP address space, offering trillions of unique network addresses, meaning that all artifacts could form part of an all-encompassing ubiquitous network.) Sony aim to work towards the creation of a new business model based on this potential.

» *Strengthening the device business to develop semiconductor and display hardware*. Sony have understood that microprocessors, digital signal processors and other integrated circuits determine not only the functionality and quality of consumer electronic hardware, but the competitiveness of their entire business model. Sony plan to increase support for its S&S Architecture Center and strengthen its capacities for system large-scale integration (LSI) development.

Sony will begin constructing a network platform – the intra-network and customer transaction network services to support group operations – by first establishing the broadband network center as one of the corporation's key technology centers. They intend to standardize the network platform elements of billing, settlement, authentication, and copyright protection on a global basis. They hope that "this will heighten customer convenience, facilitate tie-ups with related businesses and assist with the creation of an integrated business model within the ubiquitous value network."

Strengthening Internet/communication services

Further to this, Sony plan to accelerate their Internet/communication network services. The Sony Communication Network Corp launched an Internet service provision (ISP) service called SO-Net back in 1996, and currently they have over 1.6 million subscribers. SO-Net has built up a range of services and content and will continue to develop these as broadband services and content, delivered to Sony network-compatible hardware. In Japan in July 2000, Sony launched a business-to-business (B2B) broadband communications service called "Bit-Drive", which provides a range of applications and services over a wireless communications service for companies developing e-businesses. For domestic cable networks, Sony has formed the AII Corporation in association with other major Japanese utilities, and commenced digital video distribution in January 2001. This service is offered by 33 cable stations and currently reaches 200,000 households, It is planned to reach 100 stations and one million households during 2001 and Sony are continuing to explore the business opportunities inherent in direct "fiber to the home" technologies.

Sony Broadcast Media are exploring the interactive, broadband potential of satellite broadcasting, launching Sony's CS110 satellite business in spring 2002. Sony has decided to invest in 10 companies, including InteracTV Co. Ltd. With its partners, Sony will concentrate on providing interactive services, including both entertainment and financial services, which involve close communication with the user. In other words, Sony are exploring all the avenues to broadband networking, and are busy developing their entire product range to take advantage of whatever mix of broadband networking technology customers choose and making sure that there is a range of Sony-owned content and services available on these networks. To this end they intend to create new forms of entertainment to integrate hardware, content, and services.

Tooling up for "the era of 1 million publishers"

There are three main strands to this Sony initiative: new entertainment for new media – towards "100 million publishers":

» *Accelerating the development of a new integrated business model that will underpin the provision of broadband network content and services.* Sony has already developed services whose intent is to augment the attractiveness of their hardware, notably PercasTV in Japan, which relays live broadcasts (for example, images captured by the built-in digital video camera in some models of the VAIO laptop range) over the Internet. In Japan and the USA, Sony has worked with partner companies to develop the new ImageStation service, which provides new Internet-mediated ways for consumers to enjoy and "publish" the video and still images they have created on Sony digital still cameras and camcorders. In Japan a personal IT/TV product called Airboard allows easy access to the Net in what Sony describes as "home-mobile" environment. They intend to encourage the development of integrated services, content and hardware in new business models, to create new forms of entertainment and clearly recognize the power of peer-to-peer (people-to-people) media, in what Idei calls "the era of 1 million publishers."

» *Providing hardware, content and services over the Internet.* The introduction of SonyStyle.com and PlayStation.com expanded Sony's direct sales offerings in Japan, and in the USA and Europe. Also in 2000, Sony launched SonyStyle.com and SonyStyle.com Europe, and expect significant growth in these ventures.

» *Developing a PlayStation network.* Sony Computer Entertainment (SCE) is already exploring new forms of computer-mediated networked entertainment – in Japan through a link with Japanese Telecom (NTT) DoCoMo's i-mode mobile phone, and during 2001 a broadband-compatible hard disk drive unit will be introduced. SCE is also encouraging its large software developer network to create attractive content for the broadband networked era.

Of course, the secure, copyright-protected, digital distribution of such content will be a paramount concern. Sony aims to develop business models based on this kind of distribution, including initiatives in:

» *Broadband entertainment content distribution.* Music and film-video content will be digitally distributed over broadband networks, as well as through more conventional channels (through location-based movie theaters and through disk media such as CDROM and DVD). In constructing this distribution model, Sony has committed to the full protection of copyright for owners and artists.

» *Digital distribution of movies.* In the USA, Sony Pictures Entertainment is already testing a system for the distribution of digital film content, due for launch in cooperation with other content providers in late 2001. SPE's online games division is also exploring joint projects within the film business and, as mentioned earlier, Sony's AII Inc joint venture in Japan is being developed as a digital-film distribution channel.

» *Digital distribution of music.* In May 2000, Sony reached an agreement with Universal Music (a division of Vivendi) to establish a joint venture dedicated to the digital distribution of music. (This is the planned Duet service). In Japan, Sony Music Entertainment has already established "BitMusic", where customers can pay for music downloads (over 500 tracks available by April 2001). In April 2000, with joint investments from leading music companies in Japan, Sony Communication Network Corp (SCN) launched a music distribution platform called LabelGate.

Sony is planning to deliver much more than entertainment through its broadband-networked devices. Sony Bank Inc is scheduled for launch in June 2001, and Sony is developing a range of one-to-one personalized financial services for its customers, typified by Sony Life Assurance's "Life Planner" consultant system, already available in Japan. Sony Bank is a Net bank targeted at personal customers. Further to this, and in cooperation with Sony Finance International, NTT DoCoMo, Toyota, Sakura Bank and other companies, Sony has established bitwallet, Inc to promote and, from October 2001, provide prepaid electronic payment services based on Sony's non-contact smart card, which guarantees high levels of security and high-speed data transmission.

Inventing the future at Sony computer science labs

One of Sony's major resources in its quest to become a dominant player in the broadband networked "era of 1 million publishers", is its range of R&D centers. These include:

» Internet Laboratories
» Computer Science Lab
» Frontier Science Labs
» A3 Research Center
» Digital Creatures Lab
» Wireless Telecoms
» Fusion Domain Lab
» Suprastructure Lab.

The R&D labs are the wellspring from which Sony draws ideas and develops prototypes for possible new products. As an example, we'll look at some of the wide-ranging exploratory work at the Sony

Computer Science Lab (CSL), which has centers in Tokyo, Paris, and San Jose, California.

CSL was established by Toshitada Doi and the then Sony CEO Norio Ohga in 1987. CSL's first manager and current director is Mario Tokoro. Doi had a grand vision for CSL, and promised Ohga that it would exceed Xerox PARC – the famed Palo Alto Research Center funded by Xerox in the 1970s and 1980s. PARC was responsible for many developments that now characterize PC-based personal computing – including the graphical user interface, the first commercial mouse, page description languages, and object-oriented programming. Mario Tokoro became one of Nobuyuki Idei's most trusted advisors during the 1990s, and he set very wide parameters for research at CSL. Toshitada Doi describes them as "the exploration of the billions of things that could be connected to the Internet – everything from PDAs to refrigerators." CSL was to produce a range of digital technologies that would power the new Sony products when Idei took over as chairman and CEO on Norio Ohga's death in 1999. By 1998, through the work of Tokoro's CSL and the other R&D centers, Sony ranked in the top ten companies receiving US patents. Idei had a grand plan for Sony. First of all it was to transform the bulk of Sony's products into digital devices. During the 1990s, the Minidisc, DVD players, digital camcorders, Mavica digital cameras and other digital devices replaced older analog products. In the second phase, now under way, these stand-alone products are becoming nodes in a networkable system where, for example. cameras talk to TV monitors, to laptops, and to other media devices. The VAIO (video-audio integrated operations) product range is the first step in this plan, as are the home-networking products Sony is currently developing.

The core tools that Sony needs in order to deliver the networks, the robotic entertainment devices and the VAIO products, and make them all work together include a real-time operating system called Aperios, which was created at CSL and developed at the Sony Suprastructure Center. Aperios is designed to handle many operations simultaneously, so that for example, while watching a digital movie, you could pause the action to open up a movie database search engine (who was the cinematographer?), or pause a live TV commercial to go online and actually order the product, or check out the CCTV baby monitor, or take a phone or videophone call. Aperios will have the capacity to update itself with new software to accommodate an expanding range of devices that could be connected to a home network. In Japan, Sony set-top boxes running Aperios can already do more than receive and decode cable broadcasts – they can decode satellite TV from the Sony/News Corp joint venture station Sky PerfecTV!, and download music too, either playing it in streaming mode or storing it to Minidisc or other Sony device. A home area network must, of course, link devices from many different manufacturers, and Sony has developed the HAVI (home audio-video interoperability) software that has been adopted by Philips and eight other consumer electronics companies.

Later, Sony's media content holdings in video, movies and music will also be integrated into the networks, together with games networking, financial services, and other vertical Sony offerings – all fuelling home area networks and broadband network services.

Sony research revolves around the primary theme of networking. From home area networks to the "virtual society" project, Sony CSL is committed to transforming all Sony's products into networkable devices, able to communicate to each other and to wider networks. Under Nobuyuki Idei, Sony has both "gone digital" and "got wired." He is transforming the vast corporation into a Net-sensitive, market-responsive, e-business – an "e-Sony" – ready for what he and many other forecasters see as the inevitable result of converging digital media and both wired and wireless networking technologies: a broadband, globally networked marketplace. In all these initiatives and plans Idei and his senior planning team indicate that they have embraced the "network zeitgeist" and that they intend "e-Sony" to be an exemplar of e-innovation in the imminent broadband future.

NOTES

1 Nobuyuki Idei (1999) Investor Meeting "Sony's Challenges 2000", Tokyo. Online at www.sony.co.jp/en/sonyinfo/IR/financial/IRMTG/opening.html

A Glossary of E-Innovation

E-Innovation

A glossary of terms for innovation, e-innovation and new product development.

The following glossary and index of sources is derived in part from the excellent handbook by the Product Development Management Association[1] – an outstanding resource for e-innovators.

Accidental discovery – The emergence of new concepts and ideas that differ from those planned or aimed for during research.

Alpha test – The in-house, pre-production testing of software or hardware products, prior to beta testing in a wider user-group.

Architecture – In software design the pre-production process of planning the program's construction, creating flowcharts or other schematics to explain the program's construction and objectives to the development team. In distributed development situations, the architecture phase is where the program is modularized to facilitate independent development at several different locations. In information design, *information architecture* is the creation of the optimum sequencing or linking of information or content for a specific task, medium or audience.

As-is map – A process map that illustrates exactly how an existing process works. (This may differ in various ways from the published process guidelines.)

Awareness – The percentage of target customers aware of a new product's existence may be gauged by brand awareness/recall, recall of key features, etc.

Benchmarking – The derivation, from research into successful practitioners or developers in a particular sector, of best-practice guidelines to act as benchmarks in a new product or process development. In new product development, this entails identifying the best development processes and setting these as achievement targets.

Beta test – The external controlled release of pre-production products, with the objective of testing and refining the product through a wide range of real-world usage.

Bottom-up – Description of the process by which innovative or *new product development* (NPD) ideas can emerge from individuals or groups distant from any centralized planning processes.

Brainstorming – "a means of getting a large number of ideas from a group of people in a short time" a method of group collaboration that encourages problem solving through the creation of many divergent ideas.

Brand – A name, logotype, label, trademark, etc. that differentiates a product from other, competitive products in the same sector.

Brand development index – A measure of a brand's strength in a particular geographical area as gauged by the percentage of national brand sales that occur in that area, divided by the percentage of households in that area.

Breadboard – A modeling technique used for *proof of concept* that shows how the product will work, but not how it will look.

Broadband – High capacity digital data channels or networks. The many developments in broadband technologies (in satellite, cellular, telephone, cable, fiber and radio) indicate the likely gradual emergence of broadband networks over the next five years.

Business case – The result of the business analysis of a proposed new product development project, usually including financial forecasts of likely costs and profits.

Build 0– – The early development or *build* of a version of a projected software product, that can be assembled, tested and used to illustrate the proposed functioning for the development team (who may be at different locations). Provides a common model to work from.

B2B – (**business-to-business**) a description of trading operations undertaken between businesses rather than between a business and individual consumers (B2C).

Capacity planning – In new product development, the consideration of the resources (managerial, development and production) that a company needs to bring to bear on a new project.

Champion – A person (usually with some authority) who takes a special interest on a particular project and facilitates its progress and development.

Change equilibrium – The ratio of indicators and forces within an organization that either encourage change and innovation or impede it.

Checklist – A useful tool in brainstorming and other concept-generation activities (such as *mind mapping*). Designers often start mapping *opportunity spaces* or *solution spaces* by freely listing *all* possible ingredients to include in their schematic rendering.

Co-location – The location of project personnel, creative teams, etc. in the same geographical area to encourage casual interlocution and discourse, and to share common services and utilities. Virtual co-location is the aim of sophisticated broadband groupware projects that aim to replicate in cyberspace the advantages of physical co-location.

Concept – In new product development, the clear exposition of a new product idea, in the form of a written treatment, sketch, visualization, schematic, that includes its main features and consumer benefits. In other branches of design, the concept is the central idea or combination of ideas that identify a project and that will drive or inspire or otherwise inform its development.

Concept generation – The process by which new concepts are created. This can be a combination of delphi research, brainstorming, concept mapping, analysis of market intelligence, problem solving, etc.

Concept optimizing – A research method that explores how a plan-ned product's features contribute to its overall appeal to consumers. In this way, the features can be tailored or emphasized more precisely to appeal to target customers.

Concept statement – A verbal and/or pictorial statement of a (new product) concept for presentation to focus groups, client teams, or consumers. Dummies, models, demonstrations, prototypes and visualizations are all techniques used to create concept statements.

Concept study activity – The examination and deconstruction of a concept to determine any major unknowns, or potential barriers, or obstacles in the marketplace, in the technology involved, or in the production process.

Concept testing – The process whereby the concept statement is presented to potential customers/users and their responses recorded to feed back into the product development process.

Concurrent engineering – The simultaneous, or near simultaneous, or concurrent development of design and manufacturing processes, to reduce time to market. Depends on rigorous architectural design and process segmentation or modularization.

Consumer panels – Groups of consumers specially conscripted or recruited to study purchase patterns in a particular category of products, recorded using direct observation, or barcode, or other scanning techniques.

Continuous improvement – The processes of review, analysis, and iterative feedback and re-design to improve development practice or processes.

Continuous learning – The objective analysis of progress in a development project to identify actions, or changes in planned processes to improve the product, its production process, or to reduce costs, or time to completion.

Convergent thinking – In the concept-generation phase, the processes by which a wide range or divergent set of ideas are funneled and focused into smaller groups or single ideas for further development, or for more focused examination and exploration of potential.

Core benefit proposition – The central reason why a consumer buys a particular product expressed as the perceived main benefit(s) that the consumer derives or will derive from the purchase.

Creative clusters – The phenomenon whereby creative individuals perform better in peer groups or clusters. Creative clustering can be planned but often happens naturally. Finding the methods of recognizing, creating, or supporting creative clustering that are appropriate to your organization is an important step in tooling up for e-innovation.

Creative destruction – A strategy for coping with dynamic change. The essential point here is that once they are successful, companies tend to institutionalize the thinking that allowed them to thrive, making themselves targets for more agile and responsive competitors. Creative destruction is a product of continuous learning and improvement practices, and the monitoring of product lifecycles.

Critical path scheduling – A project-management technique often incorporated in project management software (such as Microsoft Project) that derives the optimum scheduling of project tasks based on their completion times and interdependencies with other elements.

Crossing the chasm – The issues involved in the transition from an early-adopter market to a mainstream market.

Decline stage – The last stage of the product lifecycle, following introduction, growth, and maturity phases.

Delphi process – The iterative and regular canvassing of expert opinion on particular technology or other developments to determine the most likely state at some future time. This technique evolved as a technology forecasting technique in the 1950s, and has been considerably enhanced by global networking processes.

Design process – The iterative development of an idea through concept, visualization, prototyping, and production to final product (or service), characterized by research and analysis, functional problem solving, information architecture, and iterative aesthetic and functional modeling, testing, and refinement.

Distributed development – A software development strategy involving the construction of a program as a set of modules that can be developed and produced at several discrete locations before being integrated by the commissioning developer.

Divergent thinking – Description of the processes undertaken in concept generation to encourage wide-ranging thinking and the generation of a large number of ideas and perspectives on a particular issue, project, or *opportunity space*.

Early adopters – Consumers who buy into products during the introductory phase of their lifecycle. Guided by their own intuition, knowledge, requirements, and desires, early adopters are the main targets of developers and designers of new products. This term is also used to describe teams or sections of an organization willing to try new processes or methods.

E-business – A description of the various tools, processes, applications, technologies, and infrastructure by which an organization can optimize or improve their business by means of ICT and networked technologies, and the process of learning from these processes and refining or redesigning organizational structures or procedures as a result. E-business is the repositioning of business to address and benefit from the opportunities created by massive networking and ubiquitous processing.

E-commerce – A description of the processes by which businesses can trade electronically with suppliers, and distributors or partners (*B2B* or business-to-business e-commerce), or sell products and/or services direct to consumers. Characterized by the use of Website catalogues, secure transaction services, and efficient order processing, monitoring, and fulfillment procedures.

E-innovation – The process of developing new products, new services, and new business structures in response to the continuous flux of competition, new technologies, and changing markets. The process is characterized by intelligence (research and *solution-space analysis*), concept-generation and concept refinement, design, and new product development and production planning, and results in the development of responsive strategies, and new products and/or services attuned to emerging market opportunities.

Engineering design – The stage in the new product development process where a product is specified in detail and configured for efficient production.

Entrepreneurial innovation – Innovation that is a result of opportunistic, rather than strategic, processes.

Event map – A chart or timeline of expected important events affecting the lifecycle of a product, used to map out potential responses to future events.

Feasibility activity – The set of tasks in which the major unknowns in a product development project are analyzed to clarify, resolve, or bypass them.

Flowchart – The graphical representation or mapping of information structures, algorithmic steps, or other processes, or procedures to provide an overview for developers and/or for clients.

Gap analysis – The examination of the difference between a current state and future desired states in order to plan for change.

Groupware – Software that provides networked, collaborative working tools for users at disparate locations, frequently including shared whiteboard drawing facilities, shared applications, messaging, diary appointments facilities, and conferencing tools. An essential component of distributed innovation and development, and for the formation of creative clusters.

Growth stage – The second stage in a product lifecycle, marked by rapid growth as the product finds general market acceptance.

Idea generation – The activities and processes that foster the emergence of new ideas that may lead to new products, new processes or new services, or to the solution of problems. Processes typically include *brainstorming, delphi procedures, checklists, mind* *mapping*, analogy, allusion and metaphor, chance, montage (bisociation), and bricolage (found objects).

Industrial design – According to the Industrial Design Society of America, the design discipline concerned with "the creation and development of concepts and specifications that optimize the function, value and appearance of products and systems for the mutual benefit of both user/consumer and manufacturer."

Innovation – A new idea, method, or device, but more specifically the creation of a new product, or service, from concept to finished, marketed product.

Innovation engine – The processes, people, and technologies involved in the creation of new ideas and new products. With its synthesis of three of these factors, the Internet itself is becoming a giant innovation machine, integrating information, intelligence, people, customers, telecommunications channels, multimedia visualization tools, groupware, and much more in a variety of collaboration tools suitable for distributed innovation and development. Open-source development is just one of the emergent qualities of such a network of interest to the innovator.

Innovative problem solving – Methods that employ rigorous problem analysis, multiple-perspective modeling of solution spaces, and pattern-breaking idea generation to stimulate innovative solutions.

Introduction stage – First stage in a product lifecycle, characterized by early adopters.

Lead users – Those companies or individuals that have defined and developed an *ad hoc* solution to a problem, a new product, or the provision of a service that is not being offered by any supplier. Lead users are an important source of ideas, and can point to a larger, unfulfilled market opportunity. Can also refer to customers who partner a developer, providing a test-user base and a real-world test bed for new products.

Manufacturability – The measure of the ease with which a product can be manufactured at minimum cost and with maximum reliability.

Market conditions – The characteristics of the marketplace into which a new product will be introduced, including competitive products, contingent products and services, sales data, price envelope, and growth potential.

Matrix converger – A tool for convergent thinking that uses a grid matrix to help synthesize and compare key concepts with numbered ratings.

Mind mapping – A tool invented by Tony Buzan and Peter Russell for mapping and understanding a complex system or process by means of spider diagrams, drawings, labels, color codes, and images. Mind maps are also good collaborative modeling tools for sharing concepts and insights. Also called *idea mapping* or *concept mapping*. An invaluable innovation tool.

Modular development – The segmentation of a software development into units that can be independently developed at various locations, often chosen for their specialist expertise, or low costs, before integration and testing in an alpha-test version.

Multidisciplinary team – An innovation, design, or product development team drawn from a number of contingent disciplines. In software/content design this can include the lead programmer, producer (or project manager), content specialist, art director or lead graphic designer, video director, animator, information architect and so forth.

Needs statement – The summary of consumer needs and requirements to be addressed by a new product or service.

New product development – The process of planning and developing a new product, from strategic planning and organizational planning, through competitive intelligence, concept generation, concept or product statement, design refinement, product and marketing plan, to production process, and commercialization of the product.

Open-source software – A software development process wherein source code is distributed freely on the Internet with the invitation for individual programmers to contribute to its development, as well as to use it, improve it or otherwise enhance it. Open source is sometimes referred to as *free software*. According to GNU free software is when the users have the freedom to run, copy, distribute, study, change, and improve the software.

Perceptual mapping – A qualitative market research tool used to help understand how consumers are thinking about present and planned products.

Process champion – The person responsible for the ongoing internal promotion and encouragement of an NPD project, tasked with evangelizing, path smoothing, and the continuous improvement of the project, as well as the building of the development team's morale.

Process map – A project-planning tool that arranges tasks (and associated developers) vertically, along a horizontal time axis.

Process re-engineering – A method of modifying organizational effectiveness by comparing an existing process to an ideal or best-in-class benchmark, then improving, modifying or re-inventing the current practice to approach this benchmark.

Product definition – A document or other presentation that defines the product concept, and may include the design specification, target market, positioning strategy, deliverable benefits, price point, and other relevant information.

Product plan – The detailed summary of all key NPD processes relating to a particular product, from product statement through to marketing plan and product commercialization.

Prototype – The embodiment of a proposed new product either as a physical or as a software model. Prototypes can be working functional models, non-working demonstration models, or complete functional and aesthetically designed models.

Pseudocode – The plain English or natural language algorithmic description of a program, often accompanied by a program flowchart.

Psychographics – The study of the intended consumer's characteristics: their attitudes, tastes, opinions, and lifestyles.

Quality function deployment – A method of relating market requirements to product development. Uses matrix analysis tables to link customer requirements to product specification.

Rapid prototyping – The process of developing a demonstration, or working, prototype with a minimum of resources and time, to prove a concept, or to gauge customer response, or to provide a common model for distributed developers.

Render – An early phase in the design process in which the product designer produces a rough visualization of a product idea. Such renders serve to rapidly illustrate the variety of approaches to a particular product development, and serve as a valuable source of initial ideas and directions for the development team to explore.

Should-be map - The result of **process re-engineering** and continuous improvement practice; a revised *as is* map. showing how a process will work in the future.

Stage-gate process - A widely used project management and monitoring process that divides a project into discrete stages separated by decision points (gates), where senior managers assess each stage and determine the project's viability for continuing to the next stage. (See Chapter 3, The Evolution of E-innovation.)

Strategic new product development - The overlapping activities of competitive intelligence, technology scoping and research, technology forecasting, market intelligence, new product development and strategic corporate planning. Helps planners identify product development opportunities, both for extending and/or adapting existing product lines and business models, and for the development of new products, and the exploration of new routes to market and new business opportunities. In software new product development, it is more appropriately called e-innovation.

Strategic innovation - The development of e-innovation strategies and methodologies by which a company can foster continuous innovation in its products and services in a more or less formalized way. Strategic innovation draws together various motivational, research, forecasting, creativity, planning, design and product development processes into an integrated strategy for innovation in response to a rapidly changing marketplace. Addressing the task both of structuring the business for change, and of nurturing a culture of innovation throughout the organization, is part and parcel of strategic innovation.

Think links - The device used in concept mapping or *mind mapping* to illustrate connections between various elements in the map of a process or the exploration of a solution space or opportunity space.

Thumbnail - The small-scale representation of an idea or visual component, often by means of a small drawing, iconic rough, or render.

Time to market - The time for the development of a new product from initial concept either to finished, market-ready product, or to first market sales.

Visionary companies – Businesses that are leading innovators in their respective sectors which become benchmarks for competitors.

Voice of the consumer – A structured interview process for *knowledge mining* customers to discover their solutions or approaches to the problems or issues being investigated.

Webcasting – The real-time coverage of an event using a Website with high bandwidth connections to the Internet backbone, featuring live video/webcam feed, live reportage and interviews, digital photojournalism, streaming audio, etc., available to many hundreds of users. Webcasts can also be archived and in this way can extend availability of live coverage through time.

Work-flow design team – The management team that constructs the work flow for projects, deciding upon the timing and evaluation criteria of stage gates, and personnel involved.

NOTES

1 PDMA (1996) *The PDMA Handbook of New Product Development*. John Wiley & Sons, New York.

Key Concepts and Resources

Resources for further exploration:

- » Approaches to e-innovation
- » Entrepreneurial innovation
- » Strategic innovation
- » Tooling up for change
- » Networked innovation
- » Mapping the opportunity-space
- » Concept generation and convergent thinking
- » Design and software design.

APPROACHES TO E-INNOVATION

E-innovation is the evolution of strategies for success in an ever-changing, technology-driven marketplace. But innovation also frequently occurs at the "outside edges" of this economy, typically emerging from hands-on practitioners – a bottom-up rather than top-down, centrally planned approach. I'm going to label these two main approaches to e-innovation *strategic innovation*, and *entrepreneurial innovation*.

But there is as yet no formalized, standard way of "engineering" e-innovation. Companies large, and small, and micro will be developing their own responsive strategies, based on a mix of the approaches surveyed in this book. There are, of course, established methodologies in many of our cultural activities for encouraging and channeling creativity. The design process is one such method (see Chapter 8), and the scientific method another, while visual artists have evolved a much less formalized approach, usually based on observation, drawing, and sketching, or other forms of visualization and model making, and sometimes using aleatoric or chance techniques, bricolage or montage. In the communications design business (including graphics and advertising), for example, the creative process often starts with a *brief* – a document that defines what is required, the audience it is aimed at, and the constraints of time, money, and resources. The iterative design process that follows is a mix of research, problem solving, proposition, experiment, testing, and refining until a suitable solution is found.

Methodologies have been developed to help spur and focus collaborative idea-generation and development, including delphi discussions, brainstorming, model making, mind or concept mapping, and their electronic, networked equivalents made possible by groupware applications and through the tools embodied in the Web/Net itself (chat, bulletin board, messaging, e-mail, etc.). The young discipline of new product development already has a range of processes, techniques, and methodologies that serve as models for e-innovation.

Kogut, Bruce and Turcanu, Anca (1999) *Global software development and the emergence of E-innovation* at http://cbi.gsia.cmu.edu/new-web/1999SFconference/Kogut/Kogut.html

Kogut, Bruce and Meitu, Anca (2000) *The Emergence of E-innovation: Insights from Open-Source Software Development* (working paper of the Reginald F. Jones Center, The Wharton School). University of Pennsylvania, PA.

Rycroft, Robert W. and Kash, Don E. (1999) *The Complexity Challenge: Technological Innovation for the 21st Century.* Cassell Academic, London.

Von Hippel, Eric (1988) *The Sources of Innovation.* Oxford University Press, Oxford.

Entrepreneurial innovation

By this I mean the more tactical approach to innovation – where an opportunity for a new product or service is identified and acted upon more or less immediately. It is typically a bottom-up approach, and while success in this arena can be short-lived and subject to the whims and ephemeral tastes and fashions of the marketplace, sometimes developments here can impact on the entire new media industry, radically redefining distribution models, creating generic new products or even entirely new business models. Entrepreneurial innovation emerges often as a result of a bottom-up or "edge-in" appreciation of a particular market opportunity, and is characterized by speedy productivization and marketing. And generally, entrepreneurial innovation does not involve considered strategic planning. It is a high-risk, "suck-it and see" approach and is most likely to emerge from small companies that are able respond quickly to a market opportunity.

Rigotti, Luca, Matthew, Ryan and Vaithianathan, Rhema (2001) *Entrepreneurial Innovation* at http://netec.mcc.ac.uk/WoPEc/data/Papers/wpawuwpge0103002.html

Small, Peter (2000) *The Entrepreneurial Web.* Pearson Education/FT.com, London

Useful links

http://www.business.com/directory/small_business/innovation/
http://www.thinksmart.com/2/whatsdifferent.html

Strategic innovation

This is characterized by the development of e-innovation strategies and methodologies by which a company can foster continuous innovation in its products and services in a more or less formalized way. Strategic innovation draws together various motivational, research, forecasting, creativity, planning, design, and product development processes into an integrated strategy for innovation in response to a rapidly changing marketplace. Part and parcel of strategic innovation is addressing the task both of structuring the business for change, and of nurturing a culture of innovation throughout the organization. And strategic innovators can learn valuable lessons from entrepreneurial innovators. I believe that sustainable innovation practice will depend on how successfully managers or creative directors can integrate these two approaches.

Brandenburger, Adam M. and Nalebuff, Barry J. (1996) *Coopetition: 1 A Revolutionary Mindset that redefines competition and cooperation; 2: The Game Theory strategy that's changing the game of business.* Doubleday, New York

Cooper, Robert G. (1993) *Winning at New Products: accelerating the process from idea to launch.* Perseus Publishing, Cambridge, MA.

Hammond, Ray (1996) *Digital Business.* Hodder and Stoughton Coronet, London.

Irwin, Roger (1998) *Management Guide to SS Tactics* at www.geocities.com/SiliconValley/Hills/9267/sstactics.html

Leifer, Richard, McDermott, Christopher M., O'Connor, Gina Colarelli *et al.* (2000) *Radical Innovation: How Mature Companies Can Outsmart Upstarts.* Harvard Business School Press, Boston, MA

McKenna, Regis (1997) *Real Time.* Harvard Business School Press, Boston, MA.

Michalski, Wolfgang (1999) *21st century technologies: a future of promise* at http://www.oecdobserver.org/news/fullstory.php?aid = 48

Moore, James F. (1995) *The Death of Competition: Leadership and Strategy in the Age of Business Ecosystems.* Harper Business, New York.

Neumann, John von and Morgenstern, Oskar (1944) *Theory of Games and Economic Behavior*. Princeton University Press, Princeton, NJ.

Newman, Nathan (1999) *The Origins and Future of Open-source Software* at www.netaction.org/opensrc/oss-whole.html

Ridderstrale, Jonas and Nordstrom, Kjell (1999) *Funky Business*. Pearson Education/FT.com, London.

Schwartz, Peter (1991) *The Art of the Long View*. Doubleday, New York.

Senge, Peter (1990) *The Fifth Discipline*. Doubleday, New York.

Useful links

business strategy: www.strategy-business.com
Peters, Tom: www.tompeters.com

TOOLING UP FOR CHANGE

By *change* I don't mean the kind of one-off restructuring that is so often a feature of management literature. I mean the continuous change that is the main context of business operations. And continuous change has always been a feature of competitive marketplaces, as Joseph Schumpeter reasoned in 1944, when he presented the idea of *creative destruction* as a strategy for coping with such dynamic change. Recently, McKinsey executives Richard Foster and Sarah Kaplan have revisited and represented Schumpeter's strategy. In *Creative Destruction: Why Companies That Are Built to Last Underperform the Market – And How to Successfully Transform Them* Foster and Kaplan present the case for "embracing discontinuity" with extensive documentation drawn from their research involving over 1,000 companies. The essential point here is that, once they are successful, companies tend to institutionalize the thinking that allowed them to thrive, making themselves targets for more agile and responsive competitors. While other management experts have visited this territory over the last few years (including Tom Peters, John P. Kotter and Peter Schwartz), there is still vast scope for innovation in innovation processes, especially in the "coopetitive" context of what James F. Moore calls the "business ecosystem" of intricately interlinked networks of customers, stakeholders and competitors. (James

F. Moore, *The Death of Competition: Leadership and Strategy in the Age of Business Ecosystems.*)

In *New Rules for the New Economy*, for example, Kevin Kelly of Global Business Network and *Wired* magazine provides useful insights into the "network effects" of such business ecosystems. But probably the most insightful and rigorous overview of the network economy is *Information Rules: A Strategic Guide to the Network Economy* by Carl Shapiro and Hal R. Varian of Harvard Business School. In Paul Taffinder's excellent *Big Change: a Route Map for Corporate Transformation* he quotes Swedish academic Goran Eckvall's "corporate climate-change" indicators derived from a series of long-term studies of corporate innovation in US and Europe.

Some of the lessons that stand out from all these analyses include:

» creating a climate of challenge, freedom and confidence;
» creating structures conducive to and supportive of new ideas;
» devolution of responsibility to the "edges" and to the "bottom";
» maximizing the value of the network;
» encouraging "creative clustering";
» continuous change requires continuous learning (a "learning organization");
» continuous change requires continuous innovation;
» encouraging play times, focused social networking, and idea times;
» building feedback and networked interactive communications channels to encourage debate;
» encouraging psychological turbulence;
» encouraging and supporting risk-taking.

Axelrod, Robert (1984) *The Evolution of Cooperation.* Basic Books, New York.

Brand, Stewart (1987) *The Media Lab: Inventing the Future at MIT.* Viking Penguin, New York.

British Telecom (1999) *BT Technology Timeline: Towards Life in 2020* at http://www.bt.com/bttj/tomorrow/index.htm

Cary, David (1996 and on) *David Cary Futures* at www.rdrop.com/~cary/html/future_history.html

Foster, Richard and Kaplan, Sarah (2001) *Creative Destruction: Why Companies That Are Built to Last Underperform the Market – And How to Successfully Transform Them*. Doubleday, New York.

Gilder, George *The Gilder Technology Report* (archive) at www.gilder-tech.com

Global Business Network at www.gbn.org

Hammond, Allen (nd) *Whichworld? Scenarios for the 21st Century*. at http://mars3.gps.caltech.edu/whichworld/explore/scenarios/scenmw.html

Kahn, Herman (nd) *Choosing a perspective on the Future*. Hudson Institute at www.hudson.org

Kelly, Kevin (1998) *New Rules for the New Economy*. Fourth Estate, London.

Kotter, John P. (1996) *Leading Change*. Harvard Business School Press, Boston MA.

Levine, Rick, Searls, Doc, Locke Christopher and Weinburger, David (2000) *The Cluetrain Manifesto*. Pearson Education/FT.com, London, and www.cluetrain.com

Mooneyham, J.R. (nd) *An Illustrated Speculative Timeline of Future Technology and Social Change* at http://kurellian.tripod.com/spint.html

Moore, James F. (1995) *The Death of Competition: Leadership and Strategy in the Age of Business Ecosystems*. HarperBusiness, New York.

Shapiro, Carl and Varian, Hal B. (1998) *Information Rules: A Strategic Guide to the Network*. Harvard Business School Press, Boston, MA.

Schwartz, Peter (1996) *The Art of the Long View – planning for the future in an uncertain world*. Doubleday, New York.

Small, Peter (2000) *The Entrepreneurial Web*. Pearson/FT.com, London.

Taffinder, Paul (1998) *Big Change: A Route Map for Corporate Transformation*. John Wiley & Sons, New York.

Useful links

Product Development and Management Association: www.pdma.org

Sunday Times "Chronicle of the Future": www.chronicle-future.co.uk

NETWORKED INNOVATION

I have already discussed (in the chapters on the e-dimension and the global dimension) how software development businesses are utilizing the opportunities of networking in distributed development and using open-source development methods, and this is one way that the formal and entrepreneurial approaches can combine. The possibilities of devolving innovation from top-down, central strategic management to the "edges" – to development teams and individual creatives, and in the creation of online creative clusters for multi-participatory innovation are other directions here. Tapping into the resources at the edge of an enterprise – to that zone where customers and clients interact with individual managers, problem-solvers and practitioners – is one aspect of this, but another is in tapping into the creative wellspring of developers and designers from which bottom-up innovation flows. Most designers and developers form part of an informal global peer group or "extranet" of cultural commerce and communication. They tap the zeitgeist of the digital domain. They are the hyper-aware "street savvy" users and critical appraisers of the infrastructure, and the products and services, and fashions-trends emerging in the cyber-marketplace. And their expertise as both makers and users, as both authors and audience, as developers and consumers of software, is so often an untapped or underutilized resource.

Cairncross, Frances (1997) *The Death of Distance – How the communications revolution will change our lives.* Harvard Business School Press, Boston, MA.

Dibona, Chris (ed.) (1999) *Voices from the Open Source Revolution.* O'Reilly Open Source, Cambridge, MA.

Economides, Nicholas (nd) *The economics of networks* at http://raven.stern.nyu.edu/networks/site.html

Himanen, Pekka, Torvalds, Linus and Castells, Manuel (2001) *The Hacker Ethic: And the Spirit of the Information Age.* Random House, New York.

Kelly, Kevin (1994) *Out of Control: The New Biology of Machines.* Fourth Estate, London.

Kelly, Kevin (1998) *New Rules for the New Economy: 10 ways the Network Economy is changing everything*. Fourth Estate, London.

Licklider, Joseph (1960) *Man–Computer Symbiosis* at http://www.memex.org/licklider.html

Licklider, Joseph and Taylor, Robert (1968) *The Computer as a Communications Device* at http://www.memex.org/licklider.html

Moody, Glyn (2001) *Rebel Code: Linux and the Open Source Revolution*. Perseus Publishing, Reading, MA.

Newman, Nathan (1999) *The Origins and Future of Open Source Software* at http://www.netaction.org/opensrc/future/oss-whole.html#create

Prasad, Ganesh (2000) *The coming Java-Linux duopoly* at www.linux-devices.com/articles/AT7102892618

Raymond, Eric S. (1998 and on) *Open-Source Software – a new development methodology* at www.opensource.org/halloween/halloween1.html

Raymond, Eric S. (2001) *The Cathedral and the Bazaar* at www.tuxedo.org/~esr/writings/cathedral-bazaar/

Raymond, Eric S., Young, Bob, and O'Reilly, Tim (2001) *The Cathedral & the Bazaar: Musings on Linux and Open Source by an Accidental Revolutionary*. O'Reilly & Associates, Cambridge, MA.

Rosenberg, Donald K. (2000) *Open Source: The Unauthorized White Papers*. Hungry Minds, Inc., New York.

Schrage, Michael (1990) *Shared Minds: New technologies of collaboration*. Random House, New York.

Turoff, Murray (1993) *The Network Nation* (first published 1978). MIT Press, Cambridge, MA.

Varian, Hal (1998 on) *The information economy* at www.sims.berkeley.edu/resources/infoecon

Useful links

3G Partnership Project: www.3gpp.org

Advanced Television Enhancement Forum (ATVEF): www.atvef.com

GNU Website: www.gnu.org

Open-Source Organization: www.opensource.org

MAPPING THE OPPORTUNITY-SPACE: SCOPING DEVELOPMENTS AND IDENTIFYING OPPORTUNITY

The analysis and assessment of new technology developments is the first challenge of any entrepreneurial innovation. The main sources of information here include the various standards-setting organizations, such as the World Wide Web Consortium (W3C), the Motion Picture Expert Group (MPEG), the US National Institute of Standards and Technology (NIST), the International Standards Organization (ISO) and the Institute of Electrical and Electronic Engineers (IEEE), and the related range of commentary, newsgroups and special-interest groups that debate and discuss these issues on the Web/Net. New standards mean new opportunities. The researcher/analyst has to be able to build both a big picture of what is happening across the plethora of different technologies contributing to the development of new media, and to be able to identify specific developments of interest to a particular client. Technical specification proposals are thoroughly debated and critiqued on the Web/Net and the researcher will also need to discuss these with in-house developers to build a first-hand appreciation of the possible opportunities that might emerge.

Buzan, Tony and Buzan, Barry (1996) *The Mind Map Book : How to Use Radiant Thinking to Maximize Your Brain's Untapped Potential.* Plume Publishing, New York. Mind maps at http://www.buzancentre. com/mm_desc.html

Kurzweil, Raymond (1990) *The Age of Intelligent Machines.* MIT Press, Cambridge, MA.

Kurzweil, Raymond (1999) *The Age of Spiritual Machines.* Orion Business Books, London.

McCann, John M. (1997 on) *Technology Cybertrends* at www.duke. edu/~mccann/q-tech.htm

Useful links

3G Partnership Project: www.3gpp.org
Advanced Television Enhancement Forum (ATVEF): www.atvef.com
Institute of Electrical and Electronic Engineers: www.ieee.org
International Standards Organization (ISO): www.iso.ch
International Telecommunication Union (ITU): www.itu.int

MIT Software Agents Projects: http://mevard.www.media.mit.edu/
groups/agents/projects

Motion Picture Experts Group (MPEG): www.mpeg.org

Russell, Peter – mind-mapping Website: www.peterussell.com/
mindmap1.html

World Wide Web Consortium (W3C): www.w3.org

Concept generation and convergent thinking

Building a schematic representation of sectors of the "big picture"
helps identify the interesting gaps, overlaps, contiguities, or opportunity spaces occurring in the marketplace. Schematics like this are
likely to be multimedia ones in the sense used by Tony Buzan
and Peter Russell in their description of *mind mapping*, a technique for illustrating and understanding complex processes, using
pictures as well as color pens, notes and so forth (for example,
see www.peterussell.com/mindmap1.html). This approach means that
stylistic, lifestyle, and other contextual information can be integrated
into a schematic of the opportunity space. The aesthetics of such
diagrams are, of course, a secondary concern. The primary purpose
of such mind maps is in their creation – the process of thinking-
through a multivariate problem while at the same time modeling it on
paper. Networked, collaborative, multimedia mind mapping/modeling
is of course the "ideal" here – paste in a spreadsheet next to that
photograph, a video clip next to this map, etc.

Buzan, Tony and Buzan, Barry (1996) *The Mind Map Book : How to Use
Radiant Thinking to Maximize Your Brain's Untapped Potential.*
Plume Publishing, New York.

mind maps at http://www.buzancentre.com/mm_desc.html

Demarco, Tom and Lister, Timothy (1999) *Peopleware: Productive
Projects and Teams.* Dorset House, New York.

Koestler, Arthur (1975) *The Act of Creation* (published 1964). Hutchin-
son Picador, London.

Garud, Raghu; Jain, Sanjay and Phelps, Corey (1998) *A Tale of Two
Browsers* at www.stern.nyu.edu/~rgarud/browserchat/strat.html

Useful links

Concept-generation software summary: http://www.smeal.psu.edu/
isbm/npd/sw_table.html

Design and software design

Brooks, Frederick P. Jnr (1975) *The Mythical Man-Month*. Addison-Wesley, Reading, MA.

Cusumano, Michael A. (1991) *Japan's Software Factories*. Oxford University Press, New York.

Hawkins, Trip (1983) "Shaping consumer software" (interview with Phil Lemmons and Barbara Robertson in *Byte*, October 1983).

Hughes, Bob (2000) *Dust or Magic – Secrets of successful multimedia design*. Pearson Education, London.

Jones, Jon Chris (1988) "Softecnica" in *Design After Modernism* (ed. John Thackara). Thames and Hudson, London.

Laurel, Brenda (1989) "On Dramatic Interaction". *Verbum, Journal of Personal Computer Aesthetics*. (3)3.

Laurel, Brenda (1990) "Interface Agents: Metaphors with Character" in *The Art of Human-Computer Interface Design* (ed. Brenda Laurel). Addison-Wesley, Reading, MA.

Laurel, Brenda (1991) *Computers as Theatre*. Addison-Wesley, Reading, MA.

Leary, Timothy (1990) "The Interpersonal, Interactive, Interdimensional Interface" in *The Art of Human-Computer Interface Design* (ed. Brenda Laurel). Addison-Wesley, Reading, MA.

McConnell, Steve (1996) *Rapid Development*. Microsoft Press, Redmond, WA.

Meth, Clifford (1996) "Invisible Computing". *Electronic Design*, January.

Michie, Donald, Johnston, Rory (1984) *The Creative Computer – Machine intelligence and human intelligence*. Viking Penguin, London.

Morningstar, Chip and Farmer, S. Randall (1992) "The Lessons of Lucasfilm's Habitat" in *Cyberspace: First Steps* (ed. Michael Benedict). MIT Press, Cambridge, MA.

Nelson, Ted (1987) *Computer Lib – Dream Machines* (originally published 1974). Tempus Books, Microsoft Press, Redmond, WA.

Nelson, Ted (1989) "The Crime of Wizzywig." *Mondo 2000*, August.

Nelson, Ted (1990) "The Right Way to Think About Software Design" in *The Art of Human-Computer Interface Design* (ed. Brenda Laurel). Addison-Wesley, Reading, MA.

Ten Steps to Making E-Innovation Work

» Tooling up for opportunity
» Opportunity scoping
» Opportunity identification
» Concept statement
» Project launch
» Prototype
» Initial testing
» Product development
» Trial implementation
» Full commercialization and creative marketing.

How do you create a successful new product? Innovation is the ongoing creative response to a dynamically changing marketplace. In the electronic marketplace, innovation is a strategic essential. E-innovation is the strategically planned process for encouraging and expediting innovation in the real-time, distributed and tightly networked marketplace. In an environment characterized by the *new*, successfully producing the *new* becomes central to business development. The *new* can turn small companies into big ones. And businesses that don't keep growing are doomed to stasis, withering, and death. We have seen how companies small and large innovate, and how innovation processes can work in both top-down and bottom-up modes (Cybiko and Sony; see Chapter 6, The State of the Art), and how e-innovation hybridizes these two approaches, attempting to marry strategic planning, product portfolio management, and a responsive product innovation process with tactical, entrepreneurial opportunism.

However, innovation and new product development is by definition a risk-taking activity. Risk can be mitigated by strategic planning, process monitoring (stage-gate process; see Chapter 3, The Evolution of E-innovation), and designing products that are built for change – or designed to be "future proof" in the same way that software development is a process of continual refinement or embellishment ("vaporware to bloatware" as they say). In hardware new product development, there are several ways of building adaptability and continuous innovation into products – borrowing ideas from object-oriented software development, products can be designed as modular entities to be networked and plugged together in different configurations to reveal new and exciting potential for the customer (Sony's VAIO range is an example of this approach), or products can be designed to be hybridized, just as Jeff Hawkins created his Handspring Visor PDA to be functionally modified by the insertion of new plug-ins – an MP3 player, digital camera, GSM phone – and these plug-ins themselves become new product streams.

E-innovation is not just a new product development strategy – it encompasses innovation in bringing products to market – the exploration, development and exploitation of new routes to market, new marketing concepts (such as the lucky viral marketing so successfully deployed by Cybiko and Netscape – and by Napster), and new promotional devices (such as webcasting and other event-led promotions). E-innovation is an organization-wide strategic planning for change, and the first stage involves creating the conditions, structures and processes to facilitate a culture of innovation.

1. TOOLING UP FOR OPPORTUNITY

Building a culture of *awareness* of the possibilities and advantages of continual innovation and continuous change has been the subject of some important work by authors such as Peter Senge (*The Fifth Discipline*)[1,2] Paul Taffinder (*Big Change*)[3] and Peter Small (*The Entrepreneurial Web*).[4] Building a culture of awareness to possibilities and opportunities can be facilitated by incentivizing the process – rewarding individuals and teams, both in-house and outsource or open source, for their innovations and contributions to innovation processes. It can be encouraged by flattening organizational structures, encouraging bottom-up dialogue, social networking, and feedback from the "edges" of your organization, and by building processes and structures that encourage the appropriate devolution of decision-making, responsibility, and budget-control, which foster the sense of ownership of a project. Project or product champions also play an important role here, evangelizing for their products through the organization, and through wider partnerships, and by encouraging and path smoothing for the development team.

To be most useful and purposeful, such an awareness to opportunity has to converge with (or be tempered by) a complete understanding of corporate strategic objectives, and product portfolio-development aims, and it's the job of project managers and champions to ensure that their teams have ready access to this corporate thinking – through personal dialogue, presentations, and seminars, as well as through intranet Websites, bulletin boards, e-mail, and newsletters.

Tooling up for change, then, encompasses the following activities:

» promoting awareness culture
» organizational flattening and devolution
» bottom-up and edge-in dialogue
» process development
» strategic planning

» portfolio planning
» championing.

2. OPPORTUNITY SCOPING

This is the process of scanning technological and social developments for potential new product development opportunities. Building an awareness of developments that may impact your business objectives entails the constant monitoring of new and emerging technologies, the marketplace, your customers, and your competition.

The objective here is to build a dynamic map of opportunity spaces – a big picture of emerging trends – which can help identify potential synergies, discontinuities, hybrids, gaps, or other opportunity spaces for your business. There are two main sources for this information. The Web/Net itself is the means for tracking and compiling developments across a wide range of relevant or contingent technology developments, competitive intelligence, market developments, trends and fashions, and so on. Equally important are your in-house resources: knowledge of your customers needs and how they actually use your products, and an awareness of the work practices, lifestyles, and dynamics of your own creative teams and individual developers. "Opportunity favors the prepared mind" is the motif here, and building a culture of awareness to opportunity is the first stage in constructing an innovation engine for your business.

This stage is characterized by divergent thinking – building a panoptic overview of the opportunity space, and listing some 20 or so potential opportunities within this space. A useful criterion here is being able to identify technologies and trends in their early maturity phase – when the technology is developed to a stage where it is ripe for future exploitation or optimization into a product or product range. The evaluation tools and processes, and your criteria for assessing this stage of technology "readiness" – that the technology is developed to the point where a product or business based on this technology could be rapidly and profitably developed – must then be built. These are the techniques employed:

» radar scoping
  » use Web/Net as scoping engine

» delphi circulars
» trade shows/conferences
» watching the edge and the street
  » keep in touch with developers, designers, artists
  » trend and fashion scoping
» customer involvement
  » customer referrals
  » customer practice
  » lead users group
» identifying initial list of opportunities (of "technology-ready" opportunities)
  » checklists
  » brainstorming
  » mind mapping
  » project selection
» mapping the opportunity space
  » mind mapping, concept mapping, matrix-building and other information-mapping of opportunities
» creating conditions conducive to accidental discovery
  » building culture of awareness at all levels of the business
  » encouraging and rewarding considered risk-taking.

3. OPPORTUNITY IDENTIFICATION

This stage involves the sieving and comparative rating of opportunities listed in the opportunity-scoping phase, based on an initial assessment of their potential readiness for commercial development. The opportunity identification stage involves ruthless comparison of potential opportunities, by taking a closer look at the candidates, and examining their technological, operational, and financial feasibility for further development. This is very much a first-approximation study. One of the aims of e-innovation is to develop opportunity scoping processes that incur minimal costs in these early processes, thereby limiting your risk or exposure.

The 20 or so opportunities identified in the scoping phase are rated as to their feasibility – the size of the potential market, the strength of other players in this market, the investment required to productivize, the "time to market" – and the implications for your strategic business development (the fit with your objectives, your product portfolio plans, or the potential for building new business models). The objective of this stage is to select four or five opportunities (annually) with real potential, as defined by your initial research. This step is concerned with:

» defining the NPD opportunities
» assessing investment risk in developing opportunity
» assessing strategic business implications
» assessing market worth
» surveying competition and other players.

4. CONCEPT STATEMENT

The objective here is to prepare a comprehensive, though short, concept statement document for the proposed projects. It should include the idea (the product, or service, or other opportunity clearly defined), outline of the potential market (including competitors, size of market, potential likely customers, and other key players), the possible partners that would be required, and an estimate of the development time and costs involved. There should also be a consideration of a number of implementation solutions – if the concept does not work as envisaged, what are the opportunities for alternative or reduced-function implementations? A viable escape route reduces the risk involved in product development. The potential projects by this time will have been winnowed down to two or three (per year). This stage of the e-innovation process is the last opportunity to withdraw from the project at little or no cost. In summary, it includes the following:

» concept statement
» benchmarking
» product definition
» process planning technology or development partnerships
» capacity planning, champion/project leader, formation of creative clusters
» market conditions
» business case
» feasibility activity

» flowchart
» event map
» critical path scheduling.

5. PROJECT LAUNCH

This marks the formal launch of a new product development project, and involves a commitment of resources – including the appointment of project manager, development team, and project champion. At this stage, relationships with any development partners are contractually formalized, and the concept is honed and polished as a result of detailed examination by partners and by the development team. Each project is separately analyzed and the single, most promising implementation approach is chosen for development. Planning at this stage will consider the technical and organizational requirements of the development process, the evaluation and selection of suppliers, distributors, or other partners, consideration of legal issues, and importantly, a number of potential *lead customers* with whom the concept can be tested and who will assist in the development process as test-users and evaluators. This stage will involve the following:

» appoint project leader and champion
» detailed project planning
» recruit/assemble development team
» engineering design
» development partners
» recruit lead customer group.

6. PROTOTYPE

The first aim of the development team will be to produce, as rapidly as possible, a working prototype of the project. Producing an early prototype has several advantages:

» as a demonstration of proof of concept;
» as a presentation to partners and potential customers;
» to provide a common model for the development team;
» as a test bed for early learning and refinement of design/production process;

» as a valuable tool for recruiting partners, or for raising venture capital; and
» to establish intellectual property rights

Of course, building a prototype is not done in isolation from the rest of the design process. Preparatory design work may include the collection and collation of media assets (photographs, graphics, textual content, video, audio, etc.), and the initial processing or digitalization of these, the design of the information architecture underpinning the program, the development of briefings and specifications (the flowcharting of algorithms or the writing of pseudocode, design briefs for graphics, 3D, animation, etc., specifications and briefs for product designers and engineers), and the identification of the major functions to be demonstrated in the prototype.

There are several software tools that enable rapid prototyping (Visual Basic, Macromedia Director, Visual Java, etc.). The prototype is not meant to be a completely working product. Rather it is to demonstrate the key features of the product, often with dummy content or blind links. For hardware development projects, there are alternatives to full working prototypes. Jeff Hawkins used a carved wooden model of the wannabe PalmPilot, and John Sculley made a video to illustrate his "knowledge navigator" idea – that was later productivized as the Newton. With 3D computer graphics and animation, a product idea can be visualized and "materialized" successfully without the tooling-up required for a physical prototype. The following will play a part in prototype development:

» initial renders and roughs
» graphics and schematic drawings
» specifications
» model making or software prototype
» contextual presentational materials.

7. INITIAL TESTING

Armed with a prototype or demonstration video/visualization, it's time to involve partners and lead customers directly in the product development process. This initial exposure of the product concretizes the concept, and provides a vehicle for examining its potential. If a lead customer/development partner hasn't been identified yet, then evaluation customers will have to be recruited at this stage. Alternatively a sample consumer group can be formed and trial presentations/user testing performed and monitored.

If working prototypes accurately model the proposed project, then the initial testing phase can provide valuable feedback – not only for fine-tuning the concept, but also as a gauge of how the proposed product will sell. This stage marks an important stage-gate prior to commitment to full development and includes:

» presentations to lead customers
» presentations to technology or other partners
» presentations to sample consumer groups
» initial user testing
» monitoring and recording feedback
» stage-gate before full product development.

8. PRODUCT DEVELOPMENT

At this stage, assuming a successful prototype exposure and initial testing phase, the product development can be continued, incorporating the feedback from users, lead customers and partners, and a concept review and finessing by the development team.

All program components, including assets preparation, original graphics, artwork and copywriting, core programming, extra programming (databases, special component applications, etc.) and media production (video, audio, animation, etc.) will be planned for modular, and where possible, concurrent production. The product development process may itself be subject to a stage-gate process, as well as regular quality assurance and user testing, and current work in progress may be made available to technology partners and lead customers throughout the development process.

The development process is open ended (software products are continuously developed), but clear aims and objectives for the first release version will determine a timeframe and deadline for delivery of an optimum product. Plans for distribution, direct selling, and the exploitation of new routes to market, packaging and marketing plan will also be prepared at this stage, prior to coordinating and testing these processes in a trial implementation. The key features of this stage are:

» distributed development
» modular development
» open-sourcing development
» asset management
» media design and development
» programming
» program-build
» packaging
» marketing plan.

9. TRIAL IMPLEMENTATION

When the product has completed alpha testing, the "soft launch" or trial implementation can be planned and carried out. Ideally this will be performed using evaluation partners, lead customers and other early adopter customers as reference customers. The aim here is to ensure a smooth commercial launch and rollout. The reference customers will receive a fully packaged and documented "finished" product (i.e., in the exact form that a wider commercial market will receive it), though of course this phase is intended both to test the product in a rigorous "real" commercial environment, as well as to test and prove the support infrastructure (distribution, software implementation support, online or physical help-system, etc.), and may induce a final "finessing" stage of product development prior to commercial rollout. The activities involved are:

» testing with reference customers
» testing and final critique from technology partners
» quality assurance
» product refining and finessing
» support infrastructure
» product process refinement.

10. FULL COMMERCIALIZATION AND CREATIVE MARKETING

This is the product launch and rollout, and involves the coordination of several interrelated activities, including production process, marketing, packaging, distribution, support systems, secure transaction mechanisms, fulfillment mechanisms, order tracking, and the like. These processes will have been tested in the previous phase and now, it is hoped, can be smoothly instituted on a full commercial basis. Close monitoring and tracking of these processes will allow for real-time adjustment or alterations in response to customers and to changing conditions in the marketplace. This final step, then, involves:

» coordinating production, promotion, distribution, and marketing processes
» monitoring rollout for opportunities for improvement
» instituting customer care and support services.

NOTES

1 Senge, Peter M. (1990) *The Fifth Discipline: The Art & Practice of The Learning Organization*. Doubleday, New York.
2 Senge, Peter M. (1994) *The Fifth Discipline Fieldbook: Strategies and Tools for Building a Learning Organisation*. Doubleday, New York
3 Taffinder, Paul (1998) *Big Change: A Route-map for corporate transformation*. John Wiley & Sons, New York.
4 Small, Peter (2000) *The Entrepreneurial Web*. Pearson Education/ FT.com, London.

Frequently Asked Questions (FAQs)

Q1: What is e-innovation?

A: E-innovation is the strategically planned process for encouraging and expediting innovation in the real-time, distributed, and tightly networked marketplace.

Q2: How does e-innovation differ from new product development?

A: E-innovation is as much about organization-wide change as it is about new product development – it's a culture, as well as a set of processes to innovate and develop new products and explore new ways of marketing and new routes to market.

Q3: What's the "e" for?

A: E-innovation is the process, and the philosophy, of proactively and creatively responding to continuous change. In the electronic speed – the light speed – of global networks, change is accelerating. So the "e" stands for electronic, because e-innovation uses computer-mediated networks to encourage distributed and collaborative innovation and development. But innovation is still primarily for and about people, so the "e" also stands for "enhanced", "expanded", "extended", "elaborated", oh, and "eureka!"

Q4: What is the "opportunity space"?

A: Imagine a big picture that shows the relationships between all the technologies and activities in our global networked marketplace and "information space". Now map on to this big picture all the newly emerging technologies, international standards, new practices and competitive developments, new business models, and new markets that are being created. Highlight the areas of interest to your organization or business – thick lines surrounding areas of great importance, thin lines surrounding those of lesser importance. This big picture then becomes a "map" of the opportunity space, and begins to illustrate the range of opportunities. You are an explorer in this opportunity space. You know your own aims, aspirations and objectives, and your own capacities and capabilities. Explore!

Q5: How do you define an "opportunity"?

A: Opportunities will arise both in the interaction between the value nets (also known as value chains) that surround each new development in the networked economy, and in the interaction or potential interactions between technologies and the way they are used. Mapping the likely frictions, contiguities, overlaps, correspondences, and dynamics of these technologies and value nets as they interact in the marketplace, reveals the opportunity space. The better the "information design" and the graphic illustration or computer modeling of the opportunity space, the more useful such visual exercises are. And the more hands-on this map making is, the more dynamic the processes of thinking through the implications of these new developments for your organization or business. The opportunities will be in those areas of intersection or convergence of your company's strategic objectives, product portfolio, production capacity and innovation resources, with the emerging technologies and their surrounding value nets.

Q6: What is a value net?

A: A value net describes the economic relationships surrounding a technology, business, or new type of product. It encompasses supply chains, routes to market, production methods, promotion, distribution, partners and other stakeholders. Opportunities for innovation often occur in the overlap or interaction of the value nets associated with new technologies, and new products.

Q7: How do I encourage e-innovation in my organization?

A: Here's a five-point plan.

» *Motivation* – Motivate the whole workforce, reward innovation, build a process that encourages risk taking and limits responsibility. Structure to devolve responsibility, and opportunity, to every level of the company.
» *Inspiration and education* – Build a culture of innovation, where exemplars and competitive "best-in-class" examples become familiar benchmarks, and where engineering and design are critically analyzed and issues of creative design and innovation regularly discussed.
» *Information* – Ensure the widespread dissemination and discussion of company strategic objectives, product portfolio planning and new product development ideas. Allow staff at every level the opportunity for "playing" with the new technologies – web browsing, desktop applications, games, chat rooms, etc. Build special interest groups (SIGs) of common interests or specialisms.
» *Interaction* – Encourage both formal and informal debate and interaction between staff, including management and senior management. Encourage product champions and section leaders to evangelize and inform on new product development and business development planning.
» *Structure* – Develop processes that allow maximum freedom to explore opportunities and that apply rigorous (stage-gate?) processes to ensure that good ideas are exploited. Link SIGs into the "creative clusters" that you build from core innovators – designers, engineers, programmers, producers. Exploit networks and the Web through accessible messaging, e-mail, conferencing and full intranet facilities to encourage the formation and growth of both in-house and distributed creative clusters.

Q8: What is "distributed innovation"?

A: This is the use of networks and collaborative conceptual and concept-development tools or "groupware", the use of open-source development techniques, and the building of responsive mechanisms for encouraging innovation in distributed (modularized) outsourced software development. Distributed innovation can be effectively deployed for hardware new product development too.

Q9: Why is the Web an "innovation engine"?

A: The Web has brought us the phenomenon of a world-around, real-time electronic marketplace. This marketplace is also the biggest library of information ever constructed. It is also a "multiple medium" of ideas exchange between millions of people. That's why.

Q10: Who should be in the e-innovation team?

A: Essentially it's made up of creative people. E-innovation teams will probably be structured around a producer (line or product manager), a technology head (lead programmer or engineer), and an information designer or product designer, but may include any of the following: graphic designer, filmmaker, subject expert, 3D designer/animator, web designer or webmaster, specialist programmers, cognitive psychologist/interface designer, art director, advertising or marketing specialist, production engineer. The team will also elect a product evangelizer or champion of appropriate status in the organization.

Index

Printed and bound by CPI Group (UK) Ltd, Croydon, CR0 4YY

Printed and bound by CPI Group (UK) Ltd, Croydon, CR0 4YY

13/04/2025

14656558-0003